Grampa's Left Arm

and Other Stories

Grampa's Left Arm

and Other Stories

*Tracing My Immigrant Roots
from Galicia to Pennsylvania*

by

Jim Tirjan

iUniverse LLC
Bloomington

Grampa's Left Arm and Other Stories
Tracing My Immigrant Roots from Galicia to Pennsylvania

iUniverse books may be ordered through booksellers or by contacting:

iUniverse LLC
1663 Liberty Drive
Bloomington, IN 47403
www.iuniverse.com
1-800-Authors (1-800-288-4677)

Because of the dynamic nature of the Internet, any web addresses or links contained in this book may have changed since publication and may no longer be valid. The views expressed in this work are solely those of the author and do not necessarily reflect the views of the publisher, and the publisher hereby disclaims any responsibility for them.

Any people depicted in stock imagery provided by Thinkstock are models, and such images are being used for illustrative purposes only.
Certain stock imagery © Thinkstock.

ISBN: 978-1-4917-0191-1 (sc)
ISBN: 978-1-4917-0192-8 (ebk)

Library of Congress Control Number: 2013914339

Printed in the United States of America

iUniverse rev. date: 09/03/2013

CONTENTS

For Paul

Far away places with strange-sounding names

Far away over the sea

Those far away places with the strange-sounding names

Are calling, calling me

ACKNOWLEDGEMENTS

Many thanks to Eddie Bauer, a long-time Haycock resident, who provided much useful old and new information about the area. Thanks also to Margie Goldthorp Fulp and Karina Sturman Rilling at the Haycock Historical Society for their support of this project.

In writing this book I was glad to reconnect with my Uncle Joe Schmidt, whom I remember in the book as 'Smitty', and my cousins Larry Bobiak, Ed Tirjan and Carol Tirjan Mueller. Fortunately Larry put me in touch with an archivist at the Fabian Collection in Nürnberg Germany, who provided most of the information about Königsau, the Austrian village from which my grandparents emigrated. My fellow memoirists in Ann Thompson's classes offered helpful advice and encouragement. Thanks especially to my brother, Fred, who dug invaluable family photographs out of his attic and gave me a place to stay when I returned to Pennsylvania to do research.

I have reprinted Philip Semanchuk's interesting article (as Appendix I) about his grandfather who was born in that village and settled in the same area of eastern Pennsylvania as my grandparents. I have created the maps in Appendix II using information from several sources, highlighting locations specific to my narrative.

It would not have been possible to do research for this book were it not for two historical events that happened in the 1990s: the collapse of the Soviet Union and the rise of the Internet (or more specifically, the World Wide Web). In neither case did this result in an immediate flood of information. Over the years, however, researchers have gathered a trove of stories and historical information that would have been lost as generations died off. The researchers' work not only continues—it accelerates, as once-confidential files are opened, once-secret stories are told and books are written.

Finally, it is both a curse and a blessing to have my wife edit everything. And I mean Everything! Her recommendations, patience and prodding have been invaluable throughout this process. I wouldn't and couldn't have done it without her.

Parts of this story appeared in www.broadstreetreview. com and the Haycock Historical Society newsletters in 2012.

Thank you all,

Jim Tirjan
Campbell, California 2013

INTRODUCTION

When the third grade teacher asked each of us where our families were from, I answered, *Australia* in a tiny voice. She was most impressed because nearly every other kid said Germany. That night my mother smiled when I told her I answered Australia and corrected it to *Austria*. I never made that mistake again—but this wasn't the last time I had to tell somebody where the Tirjans were from. It happened my entire life. The problem is, I never knew much beyond the name of the country until now.

Dad would say, *We're Austrian. We're different.* I could see our family was different. My grandparents and parents spoke a German dialect different from the Pennsylvania Dutch common in our community; Mennonite girls wore distinctive bonnets and long dresses. The Pennsylvania Dutch had lived in southeast Pennsylvania for hundreds of years; the Tirjans arrived in Haycock in 1931. We were Roman Catholics: they were strict Protestants. Our family drank beer and wine. We liked music, cars and good clothes.

Different, yes, but where did the Tirjans come from? Other immigrants in our town, kids my age, Latvians for instance, arrived after WWII so they knew exactly where they were from. All I knew was that all four grandparents were from a village called Königsau in Galicia, but I had no idea where that was. The earlier generations died before I was old enough to ask them any more about it.

Now, with the time and the technology to discover where they lived before they emigrated, I have learned a great deal about land they left behind. Thanks to the web I filled some voids in my family background and have a broader grasp of twentieth century history as a result. Wars and the Depression affected the Tirjans in ways I had not imagined. *Grampa's Left Arm* is both a memoir and a history tailored specifically to my family's lives.

CHAPTER 1
Smitty's Workshop

"Chrimminy, Schwartzie, put that stuff away now! The kids are here. Hand me a three-quarter inch box wrench," Smitty bellowed from under the car. My uncle Joe Schmidt, Smitty, had just graduated from high school. Now he was happily up to his ears working on his '48 Hudson Commodore Eight in the old tractor shed on his parents' farm in Haycock. Mike and I gazed in awe at the white number 6 painted on the door.

1948 Hudson

I was almost nine the summer of 1950 when my cousin, Mike Tirjan, and I spent a whole week with our grandparents, Bruno and Eva Schmidt. Their farm had everything a boy could want: fruit to pick and eat, cows to chase and a dog that knew tricks. We loved being at the farm especially when the fruit was ripe. Mike and I ate cherries. We ate apricots. We ate plums and carried buckets full of them back to the kitchen for Grandma to can. We picked beans and peas, tomatoes and corn. Grandma made wonderful pies, cakes, dumplings and cobblers. She wasted nothing: whatever we didn't eat went into the root cellar.

We caught lizards in the swamp and camped out in the woods at the end of the cow pasture. Idyllic, yes, and hot: July weather in Pennsylvania is humid and sticky day after day. The only way to cool off was a swim but, since neither Grandma nor Grampa ever drove a car, we pestered Smitty to take us at the dam on the Tohickon Creek. He had finished high school and was waiting to join the Army.

"Oh, that Smitty!" my folks, Joe and Eva, would say, rolling their eyes and shaking their heads, which made him all the more glamorous to me. Although he still lived at home, Smitty was completely occupied with his high school buddies and only occasionally stopped by family gatherings. I had never understood what my parents meant when they rolled their eyes but this summer I hoped to find out.

Johnny Schwartz, Smitty's high school buddy, swung his feet off the workbench and tossed a magazine into a wooden box. It flopped open to a picture of a woman's naked body. Wow, I had never seen anything like that. This vacation was really going to be fun. Then, just like an old-time movie calendar, the pages fanned shut.

"Hey, how are you guys doin'?" Smitty said as he skidded across the flattened cardboard boxes which kept him off the oily floor. His face and arms were smeared with grease and a lit cigarette hung from his lips.

"I hear you want to go for a swim," he called cheerfully. "Me, too. First I have to get this trannie back in. Lend me a hand, will ya?" We leaped to hand him a tool as he slid back under the grey Hudson with yellow flame-painted fenders.

Smitty's shed was really my dream shop. Outside, old Hudson doors and fenders of various colors were strewn among ragged blackberry bushes. Inside, Amey Lumber Company calendars with pictures of bosomy women wearing skimpy carpenter outfits hung beside rusty license plates and old Pennzoil, Skoal, and Rolling Rock signs. A heap of muffler parts filled one corner. A delicious smell of oil, gas and sweat hung in the air and shafts of brilliant sunshine pierced the smoky darkness. A flyspecked bulb dangled from an overhead beam. An extension cord looped over a beam to connect a beat-up AM radio blasting pop tunes and baseball scores. There on the shelf next to the radio sat the box with those interesting magazines.

Smitty liked having us around because our picking fruit and stuffing our faces freed him up to spend more time on his car.

"It's hot," Smitty said. "Why don't you wash Number Six?" He slung himself into the driver's seat and backed the car out of the shed. "That'll cool you off."

Yes, it would! We sudsed the car, paying particular attention to the lovely yellow flames and the big racing *Number 6* on the driver's door. As he sloshed a final bucket of clean water across the hood he said, "Okay, guys, let's go for a swim!"

Smitty packed Mike and me and Grandma's dog, Shep, into the Hudson and headed out to the creek. Then he cranked up the radio and sang *Goodnight Irene* at the top of his lungs. Gee whiz, with the windows wide open the whole county could hear him. He knew all the words and when he sang *Hey Good Lookin'* his accent sounded just like Hank Williams. Shep stuck his head out the window and the hot wind blew his ears straight back. Maybe Shep was used to this speed but we never went ninety miles an hour in Dad's '40 Plymouth. It didn't even have a radio.

The water was still and dark, deep as a lake behind the slimy dam where Mike had once seen eels. No way was I going near that. I watched Smitty grab a Tarzan rope high on a tree branch. He swung way, way out, then dropped

3

into the deepest place right behind the eely dam. Oh, to be as brave as Smitty.

Mike and I hung around him whenever he was home. We wanted to know everything about him, we wanted to be him. There were sometimes exciting mysteries like the time we were playing Ramah of the Jungle, a kids' TV program, and heard loud, horrible noises off in the woods. We imagined it could be the sounds of real lions fighting. The roars rose and fell exactly like battling beasts. But the woods were so buggy and thick we couldn't get through to see. After a terrific bang, everything went quiet.

That night Smitty came to supper wearing his baseball cap.

"Take that off," Grandma ordered. "You don't wear a hat in the house."

"There's a cold draft in here, Mama," he answered sullenly. We boys watched to see what that meant because we knew there was never a cold draft in a kitchen in Pennsylvania in July.

"Ha," Grandma snorted and snatched off his cap.

After a heated argument, some of it in German that we couldn't understand, Smitty revealed he was hiding a big lump on his head. Some draft: then we learned the real story. Smitty and his buddies had cut a dirt track in the woods to race their cars. So that was the lion's roar.

The Hudson had a special step-down body that lowered the center of gravity, letting it corner better than other hot rods at the time. That day Smitty pushed the mighty Hudson a little too fast and it slid off the track, smashing into the trees. It was wrecked. But we had just washed it! There'd be no more trips to the creek.

After this exciting summer visit to Grandma's we returned home and settled back into the school routine. Sister Margie and I were asleep in our beds when the phone rang downstairs. Margie and I were all ears.

"Let's go, Eve. Smitty's in the hospital," Dad called. "A motorcycle accident. That's all I know."

Smitty had been drafted and just finished basic training. That night when he came back to say goodbye before shipping out to Korea, his buddies dared him to perform the angel stunt on his motorcycle. That is, ride fast down the middle of the highway standing on the seat, with his arms out to the side like wings. He'd often done this in daylight but at midnight, after many farewell drinks, the big Indian motorcycle hit something and cartwheeled over him, breaking his back. He lay in traction and rehab for months. The Army discharged him. He never went to Korea.

I didn't see much of Smitty after the summer of Number Six. He got back on his feet, got a job, probably bought another bike. He dated a string of beautiful women who probably looked like those calendar girls. He married, lived on the Schmidt farm until his parents died, then moved to Mississippi and finally to Kentucky hill country. Last I heard he was a pastor in an evangelical church, a role a hellion should be well qualified for. Maybe he's found his calling convincing impetuous youth to suppress their reckless impulses, and instead, follow the path of righteousness.

Boy, I hope not.

Eva and Bruno Schmidt
Haycock (1950)

CHAPTER 2

The Spy Who Lived Down the Lane

In August of '51 Mike and I were again at Grandma's farm again but this time we had to entertain ourselves. We hadn't seen Smitty since his motorcycle accident and his workshop was locked up tight, the footpath totally grown over. We peered through the dusty window at his tools and calendar girls. There was no sign of Number Six. Several old tires leaned outside against the wall.

"I bet these are the Hudson tires," Mike said, thoughtfully. "I remember washing them. Smitty won't mind our borrowing 'em."

It was Mike's idea to race old tires down a nearby hill. He was two years older but I knew I was just as strong and just as smart. We competed at just about everything.

"These aren't worth anything, anyway. Look, you can see right through to the canvas." He chose his. "Here, you take this whitewall."

We pushed our tires down a path to the newly paved two-lane road. If Grandma spotted us she might not let us borrow the tires. Besides, she had warned us not to go down a certain dirt lane—we didn't know exactly where it was—because somebody bad lived there. A spy. Nothing to do with us.

The road was beautifully smooth, perfect for a tire rolling competition. The sun had softened the asphalt in spots so we had to push the heavy tires on the gravel shoulder. Hard work, but the more I sweated, the better I liked my tire. I gave it a name, to myself only, of course. 'Big Whitewall'. The stripe looked like speed and I could even hear the roar of the Hudson as it flew into the trees on its final run. If Mike was right, this tire might be the front wheel of that very car. How far could it go? I would have to start it rolling really fast. It was already so heavy I could hardly keep it upright.

From the top of the hill the newly paved road swooped under a long canopy of trees. Way down the hill the road bent to the right and out of sight. Here the asphalt was cool, firm and dry. There wouldn't be a speck of tar on Big White. We paused. Cicadas hummed; not a single car passed. In my mind's eye, the trees seemed to form a wall like the stock car track fence I'd seen on TV.

Intent on our tires, we barely noticed we had come to the entrance of that dirt lane that led to the spy's house. Grownups had not explained what a spy was or what someone like that was doing in Haycock Township. We kids could hardly understand our grandparents' mixed up English and German but we did understand words like "FBI", "shortwave radio", "communists" and "Russia". So we knew a spy was dangerous. My father, Joe, and Mike's father, Jake, paid close attention to radio newscasters such as Walter Winchell and Drew Pearson who warned that communists and Russians would overthrow our government and enslave us. Immigrants from Eastern Europe kept to themselves.

Yet Mike told me that Uncle Smitty had said the spy was a beautiful woman. Smitty had mowed her lawn and, according to Mike, there was a swimming pool behind her house. And that this spy lady came from New York on weekends in a big car, all dressed up and carrying a little Dachshund in a purse under her arm. Smitty said she sometimes threw parties. On hot days, Mike whispered, the spy lady and her friends sunbathed naked by the pool. Mike thought we should go spy on the spy right then. He was just like Smitty, always pushing the limits. I wasn't interested in naked spy ladies. I just wanted to roll Big White. I shook my head.

"Ha. You'll see, I'm gonna beat you," he said.

He went first, of course, starting his tire down the hill as if it were a sled, but it wobbled and flopped over after twenty feet. Big White rolled down the hill, veered left and fell over sooner so Mike won the first try.

His second try rolled further but turned itself into the bushes and stopped.

On my second roll, I pushed Big White further before I let it loose. Mike's had gone faster but neither one made it beyond fifty feet. As I sized up the situation for the third try, I saw that the road's slight crown was throwing the tires off. To reach that distant right bend, Big White had to stay just to the right of the centerline.

Mike's tire went almost all the way down on the third try. I lined Big White up and gave it my all on exactly the best track, just off the crown. Big White rolled straight and steady, faster, upright. I held my breath as it flew down the smooth asphalt and made a graceful swoop at the bend. This was highly satisfying.

But at that very moment, a hotrod appeared around the bend heading right at my tire. My heart stopped. *Whump!* The tire struck the front bumper, sailed straight into the air and landed on the roof with a terrible crunch.

We heard two guys holler and then we heard the sound of their engine coming up the hill toward us. In a flash, we headed into the woods. We scrambled through thickets, brambles and clouds of bugs as the car honked and the guys behind us yelled. We lay very still until we heard them drive away. Now what?

"Better not go back to the road."

"Yeah, we'll have to get the tires later."

I had run Big White smack into a car, which could have killed somebody—I could just hear Grandma scolding me. We'd lost Smitty's tires and escaped so blindly that now we were lost, too. Thick trees, scratchy vines, there could be snakes, it was a jungle. We would never get home. We would die in this wilderness.

We slogged on for hours—probably twenty minutes—until we came to a dirt lane. Then we realized that this was the lane that led to the forbidden spy's house. Mike did not hesitate.

"We'll never be this close again."

There was no sound of any cars or voices. I hesitated. He could get me in trouble.

"There's nobody around," he continued, stepping carefully forward. "Might as well take a look. She's probably not even there." I followed.

We snuck up the driveway to the tall iron gate that connected the old stone house to a big barn and peered through. The house was bigger than Grandma's with pretty white shutters. In the back a blue swimming pool shimmered in the green lawn. No one was sunbathing that we could see but there was a long, black Buick parked beside the barn. New York license plates, just like Grandma said. This really was the spy lady's house.

Our mouths hung open when suddenly a man in a dark suit appeared from the far side of an outbuilding, walking right towards us. We froze. Was he coming after us? If he told Grandma, she'd never let us come back to the farm again.

We lit out as fast as we could down the long, forbidden lane, listening for the sound of the black car coming after us. Nothing happened. We slipped under a barbed wire fence and headed off into a grassy field with big boulders to hide behind. Then I recognized where we were.

"Hey, this is Grandma's cow pasture." We were safe. "Her house is right over there."

"We can say we were just tending the cows," Mike said. "Our alibi." We decided this was better than saying we were playing in the hayloft of the barn, our favorite pastime, because we weren't supposed to do that either. Tending the cows was sort of like doing chores.

No sooner had we had settled into Grandma's familiar kitchen when the hotrod pulled into the yard. Now we were sunk. But no, it was Johnny Schwartz, Smitty's old pal, the one who liked girly magazines, and he had both tires in the back seat.

"You guys, what'd you run for?" He laughed. The whitewall was actually his. If we hadn't run off, he and the other guy would have joined our competition. "But we couldn't catch up with you."

Johnny Schwartz couldn't imagine how close we had come to getting captured by the spy or the man in that big black car. We put the tires right back where we found them. We didn't even need an alibi. Grandma never knew we had borrowed them. We never told anyone about our exciting adventure. Only later did I find out that the spy lady was the real thing.

CHAPTER 3
Hede Massing

I remember that summer more than sixty years ago because it thrilled me to think a mysterious Austrian spy lived so close to Grandma Schmidt's. This tantalizing mystery bubbled to the surface when in 2012 I asked longtime resident and Haycock historian, Eddie Bauer, if a spy had really had lived in that house. He knows everybody who lives in Haycock and many who came before. Eddie assured me Grandma was right: there really was a spy living in that house and her name was Hede Massing. What was a spy doing in Haycock? I began to dig.

There is a lot of material about this woman in Congressional records, news accounts, descriptions of Massing in biographies and in her own memoir, *This Deception* (1951). I still feel a thrill when I think how close we two country boys came to the Cold War by rolling tires and getting lost in the woods.

Hede Massing was, by her own testimony, a Soviet agent. She testified at the Alger Hiss-Whitaker Chambers trial at the House Un-American Activities Committee (HUAC) hearings in 1949 to avoid deportation back to Communist-controlled Austria. Before 1939, HUAC had focused on the Nazi threat but after WWII they turned their attention to communist subversion in the United States. HUAC was investigating Whitaker Chambers' claim that Alger Hiss was a member of the Communist Party. Chambers claimed Massing had told him, long before, that Hiss was a member of the Party. In the tumultuous Hitler-Stalin years, several communist organizations competed for power, often with lethal consequences. HUAC and the FBI spent years sorting them out. The Alger Hiss-Whitaker Chambers trial was only the beginning of what leftists called the witch hunts where many Hollywood writers, once sympathetic to humanitarian causes, were blacklisted as fellow travelers.[1]

---

[1] Witch hunts were not limited to the HUAC. The most highly publicized trial of the era was the Army-McCarthy hearings in 1954 conducted by the U.S. Senate, not the House of Representatives. With a thirst for ever more information and with Congressional support the FBI, headed by J. Edgar Hoover, grew in size and scope of operation. In 1975, three years after Hoover's death, the House of Representatives abolished the HUAC and transferred its functions to the House Judiciary Committee.

Stephen G. Fritz, *Ostkrieg: Hitler's War of Extermination in the East*, (Lexington, KY, 2011), p. 469-472. Communist infiltration of the U.S. government may have contributed to a lenient policy toward the Communist Party in the U.S. in the thirties but the real reason was geopolitical; Roosevelt knew the Unites States would need the military might of the Soviet Union to defeat Nazi Germany in a war which seemed inevitable. This turned out to be true. The Soviet Union lost over 10.7 million military personnel in WWII compared with 418,500 American deaths, a number that includes American deaths worldwide whereas Russia's fatalities were almost exclusively at the hands of the Nazis or Soviet officers shooting their defectors on the Eastern Front. It is estimated that the Red Army was responsible for 75% of Germany's 4.4 million military deaths in WWII.

Tapon, Francis, *The Hidden Europe: What Eastern Europeans Can Teach Us*, (WanderLearn Press, Berkeley, 2012), pp. 665-668. Tapon observes that young people in Russia today are totally surprised to learn that U.S. forces ever fought against the German Army in WWII. They are aware, however, of American lend-lease during the war and dropping atomic bombs on Japanese cities.

At the time, Hiss played a very important role as Assistant to the U.S. Secretary of State and was also a United Nations official. As the trials (there were two) played out, people around the world were riveted to the testimony coming out of the Committee room.

Much has been written about this difficult era. Hede Massing has contributed her version of the story as well. In her 1951 memoir, *This Deception*, Hede Massing recounts her life as a spy beginning with her unhappy childhood, her brief acting career and her introduction to German Communists. In 1920 she moved to Berlin with her first husband, Gerhard Eisler, an organizer in the Communist Party. Swept along with his anti-fascist rhetoric, she joined the movement herself.

Husband number two, Julian Gumperz, was an American whose citizenship allowed Hede to become an American citizen herself in 1927. When Adolph Hitler became Chancellor of the Reich in 1933, Hede moved to the United States with her third husband, Paul Massing. Hede and Paul actively recruited agents in New York and Washington. Her passport became a valuable asset as she carried critical documents to Europe, passing as an American tourist shopping for 'friends' back home as her cover. Moscow paid the expenses.

According to *This Deception*, Hede describes long hours interviewing people who would help the cause of world communism, not unlike a salesman developing leads for a new territory. The spy's life seems rather unexciting: long hours writing reports about potential spies, sometimes citizens who could be blackmailed into cooperating. She reported in tedious detail what they said, what they ate, whom they knew and with whom they were sleeping. She does not tell us if she slept with any of them herself but dedicated Communist apparatchiks such as Hede Massing at least married advantageously.

While still living in Germany with Paul Massing, Hede met another Communist agent, Noel Field, a U.S. State

Department employee. Noel and his German wife, Hertha, became close friends with the Massings and Hede and Paul bought a farm in Haycock, Pennsylvania, with Field's mother. They would care for her as Noel moved from one Eastern European assignment to another. The three operated the farmhouse as a bed-and-breakfast, a relaxing country house where they could keep in touch with Noel as he traveled with various humanitarian services in Europe.[2] His mother, a naïve, idealistic Quaker pacifist, also traveled to Europe acting as a courier but it was her son who was the key player in the Hiss trial because of his allegation about Hiss. It is probably no coincidence that their farm was about eight miles from Max Lieber's farm in Smithtown (near Pipersville). Maxim Lieber, was a successful New York literary agent, Communist Party member and friend of Whittaker Chambers.[3]

At the time of the trial Chambers was Senior Editor of TIME Magazine.[4] He told HUAC that Hede Massing had told *him* in 1935 that, when she had tried to recruit Noel years earlier, Field told her that he was already working with another communist organization in the United States. Hede reconfirmed the discussion with Field and implied that

---

[2]   Andy Pollack, *The Unitarian Who Shook Europe*, OSCAILT Magazine, (July 2010, Dublin, Ireland). Noel Field worked for the League of Nations in Geneva in the thirties where his social activism took him to Spain in 1939 to fight against Franco's forces. In Barcelona he befriended many people who would be in powerful positions in Communist-dominated governments in Central and Eastern Europe after the Second World War: Czechoslovakia, Poland, Hungary and Yugoslavia, in particular. Field may not have been a member of the Communist Party but was definitely a fellow traveler.

[3]   Allen Weinstein, *Perjury: The Hiss-Chambers Case*, (Stanford, 2013), p. 140.

[4]   Hede Massing, *This Deception, KGB Target: America* (New York, 1951), pp. 139, 152, 272-274.

Alger Hiss headed the competing organization. She said she then confronted Hiss about competing for the same prospect. Hiss implied that at a high level they reported to the same person.

Hiss denied it all and swore he was never a Communist Party member. While the HUAC did not believe him, the statute of limitations for espionage had run out so they convicted him of perjury before the grand jury. Hiss went to prison for five years. From his release in 1954 until his death in 1992, he struggled to clear his name.

After the Soviet Union collapsed in 1991, Russian archivists reviewed their files and found no evidence that Hiss had ever engaged in espionage or been a member of the Communist Party. But this initial investigation was cursory; it took only two days and did not include the KGB (military) archives. With the passage of time and more in-depth—and unbiased—searching it seems likely that Alger Hiss was indeed a member of the Communist Party in the United States and a Soviet agent.[5]

In the last chapter of her book, Massing seems to recognize the harm her betrayals inflicted on her friends and finally, herself. There were times between husbands when she felt isolated snooping on the friends she cultivated on Moscow's orders. Renouncing her spy career and the communist goal of world domination, she blames her imprudent choices on her mother who, she claims like a spoiled daughter, rejected and neglected her. But it's hard to feel sympathy for a woman who betrayed her adopted

---

[5]   Anne Applebaum, *Iron Curtain: The Crushing of Eastern Europe, 1944-1956*, (New York, 2012), pp. 50, 286.

Michael Dobbs, *Six Months in 1945, FDR, Stalin, Churchill, and Truman—From World War to Cold War*, (New York, 2012), pp. 16, 59, 87, 176-177.

Allen Weinstein, *Perjury: The Hiss-Chambers Case*, (Stanford, 2013), p. 135.

country and her innocent friends and then betrayed her fellow communist sympathizers and blames her mother.

The traitor's life is not as glamorous as Hollywood has portrayed it. In the end her only friends are the FBI agents who protected her while skillfully persuading her to spill all the beans. One of them could have been that man Mike and I saw at her house so long ago. Paul Massing divorced her and married Noel Field's former wife, Hertha. Noel ended badly. Arrested in Prague by the NKVD in 1949, held in solitary confinement, tortured, forced to confess to his Soviet masters, he was imprisoned.[6]

Hede continued to run the Haycock farm as a bed-and-breakfast, lecturing on the evils of Stalinism to promote her book. She lived in Haycock about as long as my grandmother, Eva Schmidt. Odd to think of two so different Austrian-born women, the same age, who emigrated to America. Neighbors for ten years! Surely Massing bought eggs from my grandmother.

Grandma sold her Haycock farm in 1954 and moved away. Hede owned her house until her death in 1981. In 2012 I drove down that scary now-paved lane and saw the spy house again after sixty-one years. It's still beautiful and mysterious and I'm still that same boy.

---

[6] Applebaum, Op. Cit., p. 451. Field's reputation was rehabilitated after the death of Stalin in 1954. He lived in Europe until his death in Budapest in 1970. Ten years later Hertha's body was laid to rest beside him.

CHAPTER 4
America Fever

Dad told me stories about his father's early life in America. My Grandfather Tirjan's English was good enough to tell some interesting tales himself. How did he come to America and wind up in Haycock, Bucks County Pennsylvania? Haycock was a rural township without a town center, a collection of farms and houses ten miles from a post office or store. This narrative is what I heard and recently discovered about their lives. Now it's my turn to hand on to my heirs what they said.

All four of my grandparents came from the same obscure village, Königsau, in the northeastern corner of the Austro-Hungarian Empire. My mother's mother, Eva Köster, the future Eva Schmidt, arrived alone on Ellis Island. According to Mom, she was an orphan raised by an uncle who treated her as his personal servant. If families could not afford to feed their children, they could legally put them out as nursemaids or housemaids for their keep until they were old enough to support themselves. Boys often apprenticed to craftsmen. This was a harsh custom but common in the nineteenth century throughout the industrializing world. The very idea of child labor outraged my mother because she adored her mother and was proud that she had come alone to America.

Many Eastern Europeans came to the New World looking for farmland; others came for jobs in the coal mines and big manufacturing plants. Some dreamed of making enough money to buy land or to invest in a business back home. But it was hard to save anything and often hard to keep a job. The Tirjans owned land in Königsau and were farmers who raised grain and bred horses for the Austrian Army.

But there was nothing for Jacob to inherit with several older brothers in line before him. To improve his prospects, his father sent him to a technical school in Vienna where he learned the machinist's trade. Machinists' cut, drilled, ground and polished the steel for the railroads, shipbuilders and the new automobile industry.

Between 1880 and 1914 at least 7.5 million people migrated from Eastern Europe to the U.S. and many settled near the East Coast cities where their ships landed. More than 25% returned: the streets of America were not paved with gold but my grandparents stayed. Coming or going American Fever[7] struck everyone. A study of emigration from one Galician village at the turn of the century found that the more property a man had, the more likely he would be to emigrate. If he already owned land, he wanted even more. America Fever promised a chance to bring home a fortune. The opposite was also true: he couldn't go back to face his village *unless* he'd made a fortune.

By 1890 coal-powered steamships which replaced the old slow and dangerous sailing vessels ran on reliable, scheduled crossings from European ports. Shipping companies dispatched agents across Europe to sell tickets to fill their steerage holds. In steerage, passengers slept and cooked in the filthy, heaving bottom of the ship and were not allowed on deck for fresh air until the ship landed. First class passengers would never lay eyes on them and for generations earlier arrivals looked down their noses at those who came in *steerage*.[8] But America Fever, reports of high

---

[7] Mark Wyman, *Round-Trip to America: The Immigrants Return to Europe 1880-1930*, (Ithaca, 1993), pp. 9-12.

[8] Edward A. Steiner, *On the Trail of the Immigrant*, (New York, 1906), pp. 30-47. The twelve-day Atlantic crossings at the time

wages and no military conscription into the armies of the King or Kaiser, like gold fever in California in 1849, made it all worth it. And why not? The agent knew all the train connections and might arrange a job at the dock as well. He could also offer return passage for a price. American manufacturers were delighted to have this steady supply of cheap labor to keep production costs low.[9]

In Europe and England, skilled workers, descendants of the guilds that closely held their expertise, were inspired by revolutionary political writings. By the time of WWI, workers' union movements, well underway in Europe and England, grew in the United States. Corporation owners resisted, as always: they locked workers out and developed new tools and processes requiring fewer skills. Unskilled workers had to take what they could get.

After completing his training in Vienna, my grandfather traveled to Germany where he may have worked until he sailed from Hamburg in 1905. Thousands of unemployed young people from neighboring countries were drawn to Germany's factories and mines at the time. He likely learned from fellow machinists where the jobs were in the United States or he may have known someone from Galicia who was already there. Germans would have been glad to see them go because they diluted the local labor market. Jacob could not know then it was not so different in America: desperate,

---

were terrible ordeals. Steiner, concludes, "On the whole, the modern passenger ship ought to be condemned as unfit for the transportation of human beings; and I do not hesitate to say that the German companies, and they provide best for their cabin passengers, are unjust if not dishonest towards the less fortunate. Take for example, the second cabin which costs about twice as much as steerage and sometimes not even twice as much yet those passengers have six times as much deck room, are much better located and are well protected against inclement weather." (note: Quote has been reworded to make it more understandable.)

[9] Wyman, Op. Cit., pp. 22-32.

unemployed workers stood outside American mill gates or lined the work areas like spare parts, taunting men lucky enough to have jobs. It was in just this hellish environment at Baldwin Locomotive Works in Eddystone, fifteen miles southwest of Philadelphia, that my grandfather found work as a machinist.

The new arrivals usually settled with people who shared their language, their religion and sometimes even came from the same hometown. The Eddystone/Chester area was a mix of Germans, Poles, Ukrainians, Russians, Greeks, Italians and Irishmen and American-born Negroes; although some had fought in both the Revolutionary and Civil Wars, they were freed from slavery only forty years before. My grandfather told me the blacks in Chester when he arrived were polite and kept to themselves.

Newcomers lived in boardinghouses, sharing rooms, even beds, and eating suppers together. Women worked in garment factories or, if the couple rented a house, took in boarders themselves. When an exhausted mill worker returned from his shift, he would to fall into a bed just vacated by someone getting up for his. The work-week was six twelve-hour days.[10] Men, far from family, had no money to spend on drink or women for company and they outnumbered women.

Anna Kaufold from Königsau landed at Ellis Island in 1910. She was just twelve when Jacob left for America and several years younger when he left for Vienna. I wish I knew if they had fallen in love or even known each other in Königsau. Did she come to marry him? Or did Annie's brothers in Philadelphia arrange the marriage? Call me romantic: a 1939 plat shows a Kaufold family living across the street from the house where my grandfather grew up, but there were several families named Kaufold in the village

---

[10]   Thomas Bell, *Out of This Furnace: A Novel of Immigrant Labor in America*, (Pittsburgh, 1976), pp. 150-153.

by then. Who knows what the family relationships may have been thirty years earlier?

The couple married in 1912 and in December Jacob Jr. arrived, followed in 1916 by my father. Aunt Elizabeth came along in 1922. From the time Jacob Sr. and Annie first set up house in 1912 until their first grandchild was born in 1936 they moved fourteen times, quite a difference from Königsau life where a family lived in the same house for generations.

Jacob and Annie Tirjan Wedding
Philadelphia (1912)

CHAPTER 5
Grampa's Left Arm

In August 1911, in Coatesville, Pennsylvania, thirty-five miles from where Annie and Jacob Tirjan lived, an angry white mob lynched a black man. Even closer to home a lynch party broke down the Chester jailhouse door to get at two blacks. Over the previous ten years more than 1,000 southern black laborers and even more whites from southern and eastern Europe arrived for jobs at Baldwin Locomotive and steelmakers Lukens and Worth Brothers. Too desperate to press for higher wages, they took whatever jobs they were offered.[11] White, black, Hungarians and Italians promoted and protected their own as best they could.

When war broke out in Europe in 1914, President Woodrow Wilson refused to send American troops to help England and France fend off the Germans. But in May 1915, when a German submarine sank the Lusitania with Americans on-board, anti-German sentiment in the United States exploded. German-American schools were closed. Even use of the term 'German-American'

---

[11] Dennis B. Downey and Raymond M. Heyser, *No Crooked Death: Coatesville, Pennsylvania and the Lynching of Zachariah Walker*, (Urbana, 1991)

suggested disloyalty and became unacceptable.[12] The Justice Department developed a list of 480,000 German aliens; in 1917-1918 alone 4,000 German-Americans were imprisoned.[13] To prove their loyalty to the U.S., German speakers were pressured to buy American War Bonds. Yet, through it all, a chilly diplomacy prevailed between the United States and Germany that lasted until American troops began arriving in France in 1917.

In October 1917 the Bolsheviks overthrew the Romanov monarchy and the Russian army pulled back from the Eastern Front. Civil war erupted between Bolshevik 'Red' and monarchist 'White' Russians. After a time, the Communist Party stole the revolution and came to power. At the same time American business leaders believed communists were infiltrating the U.S. labor movement and attempting to undermine the war effort. Since the threat of deportation hung over all foreign-borns, Austrian nationals Jacob and Annie would rarely speak German in public during and after the war.

Units of all-black soldiers fought on the Western Front in the Great War, intentionally seeking dangerous assignments to prove their courage and loyalty. But when the war ended, black veterans returned to find America was as segregated as ever. During the Red Summer of 1919, the Ku Klux Klan lynched 83 blacks and killed many more in Chicago, Washington, Philadelphia and around the country. Mitchell Palmer, the U.S. Attorney General, ordered the head of the Justice Department's new Enemy Alien Bureau, J. Edgar Hoover, to monitor and disrupt any domestic radical movements.[14]

---

[12] John Higham, *Strangers in the Land: Patterns of American Nativism, 1860-1925,* (1955) online text, p. 198.

[13] John Hawgood, *The Tragedy of German-American,* (New York, 1970)

[14] Cameron McWhirter, *Red Summer: The Summer of 1919 and the Awakening of Black America,* (New York, 2011)

The Palmer Report found Negro unrest in America was indeed part of a plot by Catholics, Jews and Eastern European foreigners to overthrow the government. Anyone could be suspect, especially Catholic, foreign-born and German-accented aliens like Jake and Annie Tirjan.

When we asked Grampa Tirjan about his gnarled left arm he told us that American and British soldiers called Germans *Heinie*, short for Heinrich, the same way everybody called Americans *Yanks*. Even his co-workers called him *Heinie* because of his accent. This infuriated him because he wasn't any *Heinie*, he was Austrian, he insisted. Most immigrants wore ugly nicknames. In spite of these insults, he loved his work setting up the precision cutting and grinding machines that produced Baldwin's locomotive drive gears.

One morning, he told us wide-eyed grandchildren, he was adjusting the clamps on a milling machine when two men, loitering along the wall and hoping for a job opening, jeered at him.

"Go back where ya came from, Heinie!"

"Lose the war, Heinie?"

"We're gonna get ya, Heinie!"

Maddened, Grampa stayed focused on the final grind of a huge gear until nature called. Very aware he'd be docked for every minute he wasn't on the shop floor and that the foreman might replace him, he hurried back. But when he returned, the massive platform began to slide sideways. Instinctively he grabbed to steady it but he was no match for the weight. The clamps had mysteriously loosened. The platform trapped his left arm, crushing it.

CHAPTER 6
Kill Me!

The last thing Jacob Tirjan remembered was the heavy platform slowly sliding sideways and foolishly reaching to stop it. Then the terrible pain and then nothing else. He tried to flex his fingers but they were numb. And he couldn't move at all because his body was strapped under the sheets.

"How are you feeling, Jacob?" the doctor asked. "It took a while to get your arm out of the machine."

"How bad is it?"

"Crushed. I can't save it."

"You mean you're going to cut my arm off?"

The doctor nodded solemnly. "Right away. Sorry. There isn't much time."

"No, don't take my arm. I have a family to support—I can't earn a living. You might as well kill me first."

My Dad loved to tell this story. "And the last thing he remembered was somebody putting the ether mask over his face."

Grandma Annie begged the surgeon to save his arm and he did, although it was too mangled to reconstruct. Eventually it healed, badly deformed and useless. It shamed him. Because the skin never recovered he wore long-sleeved shirts, even in summers.

Yet he knew he was better off than the shot-up, legless veterans in his ward. He could still use his technical training, somehow. But he wouldn't get his good job at Baldwin back, not as a cripple.

When he got out of the hospital, he was dead broke. Hearing there was machinist work at the Lima Locomotive Works in Lima, Ohio, a boomtown in the '20s, Jacob moved the family west. A Midwestern rail hub served by eight railroads, Lima was surrounded by the oil and automobile industries. The Locomotive Works built the Lima A-1 "Berkshire", the prototype for modern steam locomotives. Although Jacob found work, prejudice against foreigners ran strong; the Tirjans were not citizens and still had those accents.

Lima was the center of the notorious Black Legion, a Klan so powerful that its annual parade and rally in August 1923 drew an estimated crowd of 100,000, resulting in 3,700 new members.[15]

Then there were the Prohibition gang wars. The Federal Bureau of Investigation, under J. Edgar Hoover, hunted bootleggers and raided speakeasys. European immigrants — especially those from Catholic countries — liked their wine and beer and found the law prohibiting alcohol at celebrations and religious ceremonies ridiculous. Prohibition was driven primarily by Protestants in the south and Midwest and it was risky to buy alcohol in the rural, inland Bible Belt. If you did, you risked arrest and knew at some level you were supporting organized crime. You had to be certain to buy only from people you trusted or make your own, hoping your neighbors didn't report you.

Grampa and Grandma were afraid to raise their children in Lima. Exhausted, they moved back to the familiar Eddystone. They could not have returned to Königsau even if they could have afforded it because Galicia had

---

[15]   *Lima Republican-Gazette*, Lima, Ohio, August 3, 4 and 5, 1923.

become part of Poland.[16] Back in Pennsylvania, in 1927, forty-one-year old Jacob Tirjan Sr. became a naturalized U.S. citizen at last; Annie was naturalized two years later. My father, born a citizen, was eleven years old.

Citizens, yes, but they had a family to feed. This was a particularly painful time for Annie. She emigrated to America with enough Austrian Kronen to invest in a business. However, by the time she was finally ready to invest after Jacob lost his job at Baldwin and they had moved to and from Lima, the Kronen was worthless.[17]

So Annie rented rooms and fed boarders. She was a very fine cook. Years later some of these boarders followed her to the country for her wonderful holiday dinners and I remember very lively conversations, mostly in German, at them.

My favorite guest was Chollie Zimmith, a big Polack, irreverent, witty, totally bald as I recall. Chollie was the family's strong man when they lived in Eddystone, near Philadelphia. He knew how to buy liquor during Prohibition; perhaps he had a connection to Irving Wexler, a Polish-Jewish immigrant who bossed the Philadelphia mob. Better known by his Mafia handle, Waxy Gordon, Wexler was part of the tough, urban Jewish mob that transformed the Sicilian Mafia into a lucrative business operation during Prohibition.[18] Gordon became rich running bootleg

---

[16] They had no way to know but not going back was by far the best thing they could have done. An overview of what happened in Galicia after they left is presented in Chapter 20.

[17] T. J. Sargent, *Rational Expectations and Inflation*, (New York, 1986)

[18] Leo Katcher, *The Big Bankroll. The Life and Times of Arnold Rothstein*, (New York, 1994), pp. 226-264. The Mafia, or Cosa Nostra, had its roots in Sicily in the mid nineteenth century and came to America with its native sons. The activity of these American thugs was mostly turf wars between rival groups engaged in gambling and prostitution. But when the Volstead Act made alcohol illegal in the U.S., it was first or second generation Jews from Eastern

operations in Pennsylvania and New Jersey for the big New York crime boss, Arnold Rothstein. Rothstein ran breweries, distilleries, speakeasies, gambling halls and brothels and imported whiskey from Canada, Cuba and Europe. In fact, you can buy Gordon's Gin in any liquor store today. We never knew if Chollie was in cahoots with the Gordon mob but if my grandparents had to choose between having the corrupt Philadelphia Police[19] or Chollie Zimmith protect them, they'd pick Chollie every time.

But even strong men couldn't protect Jacob's family from polio epidemics. Polio killed by paralyzing the lungs and took a terrible toll on children until Jonas Salk developed a vaccine in 1955. Until then there was no known cause or cure. The primitive therapy was to isolate the patient from everyone, even his family. When my Uncle Jake, Jakie, came down with the dreaded disease, his parents followed the doctor's orders and moved to the country, this time sixty-five miles north of Eddystone to upper Bucks County. For two years their dear Jakie lived in a corncrib summer and winter, alone and apart. A corncrib is an open-slatted shed used for drying corn. Of course, it was bitterly cold. But Jakie lived, blind in one eye with a partial paralysis, but not enough to prevent him from fathering six children, surviving polio with his important parts intact.

Europe, the Jewish Mob, who bankrolled these existing toughs to expand into the far more profitable businesses of importing booze and dope. Other early Jewish Mob kingpins were Dopey Benny Fein and Meyer Lansky. Another, Moses "Moe" Annenberg, owner of *The Philadelphia Inquirer*, was sent to jail for tax invasion and died in prison. His only son, Walter, became the famous publisher, philanthropist and political associate of Ronald Reagan.

[19] Hans Schmidt, *Maverick Marine: General Smedley D. Butler and the Contradictions of American Military History*, (Lexington, Kentucky, 1998), pp. 144-160.

CHAPTER 7

Hoover Flags

As he entered eighth grade in 1929, my father looked forward to high school the following year. But when the stock market crashed that October he gave it up and got a job. Jakie never cared about high school but my father certainly did and resented having to work. He always felt a lack of a formal education held him back from good job opportunities. I had it pretty soft compared to him, he reminded me many times. I took those stories to heart; I recall one in particular.

By the end of Herbert Hoover's presidency in 1932, at the deepest part of the Depression, unemployment hit 25%. In some industries it reached 100%. Ships on the Delaware River grew barnacles and able-bodied men waited in bread lines. To show how desperately broke they were, men turned their pants pockets inside out, derisively calling them 'Hoover Flags'. Cardboard shacks of 'Hoover Hotels', clustered into 'Hoovervilles' in parks, on railroad sidings and under bridges in nearly every city in the country.

Bad as it was in America, it was worse in Germany. The WWI reparation payments demanded of Germany were impossibly high and Germany was broke. German war veterans demanded government action. The victorious United States, France and England, granted Germany some small relief in 1924 and again in 1929 but Germany could not even meet the reduced payment schedule.[20] Starvation spread and discontent made Germany ripe for Hitler's rise to power.

American veterans, many of them out of work since the start of the Depression, also pressed for early payment of their promised wartime bonuses—which were not due until 1945.[21] When Congress refused, seventeen thousand veterans with their wives and families marched on Washington, D.C. This Bonus Army camped in tents and shacks—a large Hooverville—on the Anacostia flats across the river from Capitol Hill and the White House.

"1945! Hell, we'll be dead by then. We need our money now!" A sympathetic House of Representatives passed the Bonus Bill to make the payments due immediately but the Senate killed it by a wide margin. It was an election year.

As the veterans waited for President Hoover to act, newspapers and radio commentary inflamed American public opinion. How could the government treat its own

---

[20] In fact Germany did not make the last payment until October 3, 2010, ninety-one years after the Treaty of Versailles formally ended WWI. The date is significant because it was the twentieth anniversary of German reunification.

[21] Each veteran was to receive a dollar for each day of domestic service, up to a maximum of $500, and $1.25 for each day of overseas time, up to a maximum of $625 (2010: $7,899). By comparison, according to the U.S. Bureau of Labor Statistics, "the average number of hours worked per week in 1919 was 45.6 and the average earnings per hour were 56.1 cents so the average weekly earnings were, therefore, $25.61."

The bonus was about 27% of what men earned who had avoided the draft yet the vets had to wait until 1945 to collect their money. A draftee was also paid a $30 monthly salary while in the service but half that amount was withheld from his salary to support his dependents and another $6 was taken for what amounted to insurance. At the end of the month, the doughboy had less than $9 left—with which he was strongly pressured to buy Liberty Bonds. Most soldiers got no money at all on paydays.

soldiers and their families so badly? The U.S. Postal Service even issued a 'Cinderella Stamp' to show its solidarity with the marchers.

Hoover directed the Washington Police to remove the encampment but the Bonus Army didn't budge. Two veterans died in the skirmishes. Fearing riots, Hoover then ordered General Douglas MacArthur to do what the Washington Police couldn't. MacArthur directed General George Patton to evict the veterans and their families and remove their tents and shacks. When the veterans saw Patton's units with cavalry and six battle tanks approaching, they greeted them with open arms believing it was a show of support for their cause. It was not. Patton ordered a cavalry charge, followed by infantry with fixed bayonets and adamsite gas, an arsenic-based vomiting agent.

Word of the U.S. Army attacking its own war veterans in the nation's capital spread across the country. Government workers in Washington poured out of their offices and lined city streets shouting, "Shame! Shame!" at Patton's troops as men, women and children ran for their lives. Army troops entered the Hooverville, marched the veterans to the train station and torched their shacks and tents. Fifty-five Bonus Army vets were injured, 135 arrested, one wife miscarried and a twelve-week-old baby died of tear gas exposure. That night Patton's army packed the protesters into boxcars in a scene foreshadowing Hitler's mass arrests and evacuations a decade later.[22] Washington residents heard the vets' screaming and pounding on locked doors as the trains pulled out of Union Station.

After this highly publicized disaster, to no one's surprise, Hoover lost the 1932 election to Franklin Roosevelt but the veterans still did not get their bonus money. They had to wait another four years for it. This would not be

---

[22] Edwin Black, *IBM and the Holocaust: The Strategic Alliance Between Nazi Germany and America's Most Powerful Corporation*, 2001, pp. 375-390.

the last time, however, that MacArthur would defy his Commander-in-Chief.

My grandfather told us the Bonus March story many times. He said he left Europe to find work in the U.S. because of the political upheavals in Austria, Germany and Russia. The year before he left, Russia's Imperial Guards opened fire on protesters in St. Petersburg and nine years later the Russian people overthrew the Czar. Grampa said the fact that MacArthur disobeyed the President's orders to stop attacking the veterans was an indication that some people in government feared an event like the Bonus March might trigger a overthrow in the United States, too.

The Bonus March was the hottest topic at every family dinner where politics trumped everything else. There was never agreement on any subject but you could always count on a good rant about MacArthur at every get together. On him, there was unanimity: he was an opportunist, a braggart and a tool of big business. They scoffed at his grandiose "I shall return!" pledge when he pulled his troops back from the Philippines in 1942 and then refused FDR's orders to modify it to "We shall return." They praised Truman for firing him when he invaded North Korea against the President's specific orders, bringing China into the Korean War and causing thousands of additional American and Korean deaths.

But invariably this would lead to a tirade about how MacArthur crushed the Bonus Army to save money for the Senate's business friends in an election year. That MacArthur became the Chairman of the Board of Remington Rand Corporation when he 'retired' only reinforced their disgust. Remington made more than typewriters; the company was a major supplier of rifles and handguns to the U.S. military and its counterparts in other countries throughout its long history.[23]

In August 1931, with the economy showing no signs of improving, my grandparents and their three children left Eddystone for good. Jobs in Eddystone, Chester and Philadelphia had disappeared along with paying boarders. Annie's brothers had moved away—three back to Galicia and one to Canada. This time Jacob and Annie Tirjan bought a farm that reminded them of long-ago Königsau. My father did not want to leave his city friends and his mother hated to leave her faltering business. She never wanted a rural life when she came from Austria. If her money hadn't disappeared, she would have bought a business in Eddystone. It wasn't really a city but it was much better than Haycock, Bucks Country, Pennsylvania.

---

[23] It still is. In 2012, Remington won the U.S. Army contract to manufacture 24,000 M4A1 carbines at $673 per unit worth a total of $16,163,252. In 2007, Remington Arms was purchased by Cerberus Capital Management and rolled into the Freedom Group.

CHAPTER 8

The Fighting Quaker

There may have been more to crushing the Bonus Army than many people realized at the time. At least that's what the men in my family claimed in their heated political discussions. Women and children were excluded—well, actually, they politely excused themselves—from these drawn-out sessions but I often hung around until I got shooed away or the men started speaking German. These loud roundtables often lasted long into the evening.

I'm sure they got most of their information from the radio. I became hooked on the strange-sounding names—Gabriel Heatter, Drew Pearson, Al Smith, Huey Long, Father Coughlin, Smedley Butler and others—but didn't know who they were. Once in a while, in addition to these names, English words like 'crooks', 'corrupt', 'almighty dollar' or 'dirty bastards' slipped out so that early on I understood where the Tirjans came down on political issues.

I recently came across Smedley Butler's name doing research on the Bonus Army. I remember being amused the first time I heard the name 'Smedley' sixty years ago. I don't think I've heard it since, but now I understand why it came up so often back then.

Smedley Butler had a radio program on WCAU in Philadelphia in the 1930s and had been Director of Public Safety (Police and Fire) in Philadelphia in 1924 and 1925.

His father, Thomas S. Butler, was my grandparents' U.S. congressional representative when they lived in Eddystone. Although the West Chester Butlers were Quakers, they played significant roles in the military. Smedley's grandfather fought with distinction in the Civil War and his father served in congress for thirty-one years until his death in 1928. Smedley was the most highly decorated Marine, the youngest Major General—and probably its biggest booster—in its history when he retired three years later.[24]

In his retirement, however, General Butler had a change of heart. He came to believe that wars were fought mostly by poor young men who bled and died on foreign soil to protect American business investments. The academy-trained brass, swivel-chair Admirals he called them, received most of the military rewards. Butler himself hadn't gone to college. He loved to speak his mind to the rank and file who packed V.F.W. halls, Quaker meetinghouses, auditoriums, theaters and fire halls. He was rough, a man of the people, like the soldiers he loved. But it was his fiery speech at the Anacostia flats encampment in support of the Bonus Army that got the attention of some powerful business interests.

Speaking around the country and on his radio program, General Butler claimed that intermediaries representing American corporations such as DuPont, J. P. Morgan, U.S. Steel, Goodyear, Standard Oil, Mutual Life Insurance, Singer Sewing Machine and the American Liberty League had approached him with a plan to overthrow

---

[24] In his thirty-four year career he had received sixteen medals, five for heroism. These included two Congressional Medals of Honor, the Marine Corps Brevet Medal, French Order of the Black Star, Navy and Army Distinguished Service Medals and humanitarian awards in China, Haiti and other countries. He was granted a leave of absence from the Marine Corp by President Coolidge to clean up the mob-controlled Philadelphia Police Department in 1924 and 1925.

the federal government.[25] In 1935 Butler stood before the McCormack-Dickstein Committee, a forerunner of the House Un-American Activities Committee (HUAC),[26] to answer questions about these claims. According to Butler, the plan, which the Committee dubbed 'the Business Plot', called for him to lead an army of 500,000 veterans to Washington, D.C. to force President Roosevelt to step down, reverse the New Deal and return to the gold standard. The conspirators envisioned a coup modeled on Mussolini's, which overthrew the King of Italy using veterans. Butler or Chief of Staff General Douglas MacArthur would then rule as a dictator.[27]

Butler told the skeptical Committee he decided to play along to see exactly who was behind it. He said he was approached after the Bonus March by a bond salesman, one Jerry MacGuire, who worked for a New York financial house. Butler could become the National Commander of the American Legion if he appeared at the Legionnaires' National Convention as a guest speaker. Then MacGuire handed him the written speech he was to deliver suggesting the Legion adopt a resolution that the United States return to the gold standard. This made no sense to Butler. His veterans wanted their money now and whether it was paper or gold made no difference, so he turned MacGuire down.

Over the next year, Butler testified, MacGuire reappeared at his hotels and speaking engagements. In 1934 MacGuire told Butler he had just returned from a fact-finding trip in Europe where he met with anti-communist veterans groups

---

[25] Jules Archer, *The Plot to Seize the White House*, (New York, 1973), pp. 228-229.

[26] The committee, co-chaired by John McCormack of Massachusetts and Samuel Dickstein of New York, was one of several precursors to the standing (permanent) House Un-American Activities Committee created in 1948. Rather than introduce confusion by referring to the McCormack-Dickstein Committee I have chosen to use the HUAC designation as many sources do.

[27] Schmidt, Op. Cit., p 223.

such as the Croix-de-Feu (Cross of Fire) in France and a similar group in Germany. His backers were impressed with these findings and wanted to sound out Butler about forming such an organization in the U.S.

The House Committee called MacGuire. He dismissed the conspiracy story. Any plan to topple the government was a hoax. He couldn't believe that Butler was so naïve. The Committee then called Singer Sewing Machine heir Robert Sterling Clark, one of the alleged financial backers of the coup. Clark ducked, travelling instead to Europe.

Since the Committee could not extradite him, Clark simply stayed away. The hearings made front-page news in the papers for a few days, but when no new evidence came to light or other witnesses were called, readers lost interest. After two months the committee's funding and authority ran out. The business newspapers which once praised Butler's populist appeal now labeled him uneducated and unsophisticated. This drove Butler to greater fury on his radio program, which aired at least twice a week on WCAU and CBS.

John McCormack, one of the committee's two chairmen, found Butler's story partly credible but, even so, his public testimony made it unlikely that such a plot could succeed after it became public knowledge. Samuel Dickstein, a New York Congressman, later became the target of HUAC and was found to have been on the payroll of NKVD, the Soviet spy agency.

Soon after the hearings, Jerry MacGuire died at the age of thirty-seven, supposedly of natural causes.

Smedley Butler continued broadcasting and speaking to veterans and pacifists—he was still a Quaker—until his death in 1940. His paper, *War is a Racket,* published in 1935, delivered the same message: big business reaped the rewards in wars while the enlisted man and the taxpayer paid the price[28]. To many fighting men General Smedley Butler was the Marine's Marine and nothing would ever change their minds. In 1936, Congress overrode FDR's veto and gave the veterans their WWI bonuses. Later that year Roosevelt was re-elected in a landslide.

Did big business really plan to stage a coup d'état? Or was Butler conned? And what about the men in my family? I'll never know for sure if they were taken in by Butler's story or if his claims had substance. Maybe I would know more if they had spoken in English—but, regardless, I am quite sure they didn't all agree.

---

[28]   Smedley Butler, *War is a Racket*, (London, 2011)

CHAPTER 9
Making Hay

Annie and Jacob Tirjan were no strangers to Haycock Township. In the nineteen years of their marriage they had moved at least five times from Eddystone to various towns in the area. One of these times was the two years they lived in Upper Black Eddy to cure Jakie's polio. But every time they concluded it just wasn't possible to earn money in the country. Annie had a boarding house to run in the city and she loved the hustle and bustle and the cooking. It was easy to buy the food she needed there but, in the midst of the Depression, they couldn't make it in Eddystone either. When employment dries up, city people always go back 'home'. On a farm, they could at least eat and now they had two strapping sons to help. Perhaps this time it would work.

They bought a beautiful old house with big fireplaces, a real barn and thirty-seven acres of good land for one dollar at a sheriff sale. At least that's the story.[29] Unlike Grandma Schmidt, neither Jacob nor Annie had farm experience and

---

[29] In all likelihood some cash was exchanged between my grandparents and the bank in addition to the one-dollar shown on the deed, although many farms did sell for pennies on the dollar in the bottom of the Depression. Banks at the time were loaded with foreclosed properties and often didn't want to be on the hook for the taxes and maintenance any longer.

neither had ever planned to live in the country. They were city folks.

It was a lonely life in the country for Annie, ten miles from her church, surrounded by Mennonite and Baptist neighbors. How she must have missed Eddystone and her brothers who had returned to Europe. Jacob could find no work and they needed money to pay for the school bus for young Betty, only nine. Jake Jr., nineteen, broke rocks on a road-building crew for a dollar a day as long as his partially paralyzed body could stand it. One week! So the family had to make the farm work. Grow some corn or some hay, raise pigs and chickens.

First Grampa Jake bought a plow and then a horse from 'Peachy' Kunas, a neighbor who lived ten miles down the road. Could that name be right? That's what Grampa called him and we heard his story many times. Peachy, Grampa remembered, was eager to sell this horse but Grampa was no yokel. He insisted he would pay cash only when Peachy delivered the animal. I can't remember the details and maybe I simply don't want to, but according to Grampa the horse died a few days after it arrived.

Peachy refused to refund the price of the horse; thus Grampa lost his money and he had a big carcass to bury. Whenever Grampa told this story he shook his fist and shouted, "Oh, that Peachy. I could have wringed his neck!" Then he laughed. He liked telling us that he was city boy who learned the hard way how to make the farm a success.

After the horse died, Grampa went looking for a replacement. It happened that the volunteer fire company not far down the road had a pair for sale. He had to buy both because they would only work together. And of course, they were much stronger than one could ever be.

They were sleek and healthy and well trained. Perhaps because he came from a horse-breeding family, Grampa fancied himself a good judge of horseflesh. And, after all, they were highly recommended by a neighbor, a Fire

Company volunteer, who showed him the complicated harnessing procedure. In a few days, Grampa hitched them to the plow and set the blade deep into the lovely spring loam to prepare the wide field for corn.

The Haycock firehouse was a mile away but on some days when the wind was right, you could hear the firehouse bell all the way out at the farm. Grandma Annie found it reassuring to know the department was keeping watch. Many times she had seen the Eddystone fire truck horses gallop past her house with their shining bells clanging, their hooves striking sparks on the pavement. It was a frightening but thrilling sight.

Without fail, the Haycock Fire Company rang the firehouse bell exactly at noon every Saturday so everyone in town could set their clocks and watches. One warm Saturday in May, when Grampa was getting the hang of managing his team and was quite pleased with how straight the furrows were becoming the clang of the bell sounded clear across that mile. Snorting with joy, the horses tore off at a gallop as they had been trained to do with the fire wagon. Grampa sawed on the reins and yelled "Whoa!" but it was a fine spring day and they felt like colts. The plow bounced and tossed Grampa high and then low, onto the dirt. Off they ran, like naughty children, strewing clanging pieces and parts of the plow far and wide. They finally stopped when their harness snagged on a clump of sassafras trees.

Grampa did not dwell on the fate of these fine specimens. For all I know, they went back to the Fire Company or a racetrack or someplace best not to imagine. He never mentioned getting his money back. But the farm, the farm! So there was another horse, just one this time, a balky fellow Grampa said that sometimes refused to go. No pulling on the halter, no clucking, no carrots nor whip could make it advance a single hoof. Now I know this episode can't be true but Grampa loved to retell it and we loved to hear it. Grampa said he got so fed-up trying to get that horse to pull a loaded hay wagon that he lit just a little fire just under the horse's rump to inspire him. The horse moved ahead — half the wagon's length — and stopped. The fire grew and set the wagon and its load alight.

Enough of horses! The July weather was hot and dry when a neighbor, a Baptist, loaned Grampa his tractor in exchange for a pan of Annie's fine strudel and a dozen laying hens. But even without horses, farm work is dangerous and the last farm story Grampa told was not funny in the least.

Humans have been making hay now for thousands of years in much the same way. Once or twice a summer the farmer cuts the tall grass, lets it dry for a day or two, keeping an eye out for rain, and rakes it into rows. Then it's pitched onto a wagon and taken to the barn for storage. Today machines do all the work but in Dad's day, all the neighbors — Baptists, Lutherans, Mennonites and even Catholics like the Tirjans — helped bring in each other's hay crop. Haying is a nasty job. Itchy dust sticks to your sweaty body and gets into your lungs. The helpers heap the hay as high as possible on each load to minimize trips to the barn. Someone tamps the load down as the ever taller wagon pitches and sways over the stubbly field. One afternoon it was my father's turn to ride the top.

The load was wobbly and the tractor's engine was roaring when he slipped on the smooth, dry hay and fell between the wagon and the tractor. Before Grampa could stop, a wagon wheel had rolled over his son, breaking a vertebra in his back.

Dad never complained about his back. He fathered four children, I among them, and lived to eighty-two.

CHAPTER 10

City Brothers, Country Sisters

Getting your driver's license was a really big deal for a teenager growing up in the country so you'd give your eye teeth to own your own car. Maybe city kids didn't need cars in the thirties and some probably still don't but by the time the Tirjans left the city, trolley and train service had declined because of the Depression and the greater convenience of a car. Country roads, the responsibility of towns and counties, were rarely paved and so, hard on cars. When tires went flat, you changed them yourself. You patched them yourself, you pumped them back up with a hand pump you stowed in the car. You washed and waxed your precious car to keep it from rusting. Since no automobile could go 100,000 miles, odometers had only five digits.

Before electric starters, cars required a lot of muscle to crank by hand. You may have seen this in old movies where the driver stands in front of his car and turns a handle connected to the driveshaft. The engine is stiff. When it fires the driver runs to the front seat, jumps behind the wheel, adjusts the throttle and retards the spark to keep the engine from kicking back. If it kicks back while he is still cranking, the handle can violently reverse itself and flail uncontrollably before he can pull it out. That flipping handle could break his wrist or even his jaw. This exercise took several cranks and leaps into the front seat before the engine caught. In rain or mud, in a ditch, he might never get it going. Because of his gimpy left arm my grandfather hated starting the car. Even shifting the rough gears or wrestling with the steering wheel on rutted roads made driving hard for Grampa.

Once there were a hundred car manufacturers but by the late 1920s there were only ten. Early on, Ford's Model T and Model A were the most popular because they were cheap to buy, parts were widely available and almost anybody could fix them.

But there would never be a Ford car in our family. While Henry Ford had revolutionized automobile manufacturing, when his employees tried to unionize, he brutally put them down.[30] Our family sympathized with the workers. Always sympathized with the workers.

Grampa had bad luck with cars from the beginning. Dad loved to tell the story about his father, who, preparing to move to the country, in spite of the family's reluctance, bought a used car at what he believed was a reasonable price. It purred out of the lot and down a long hill, then quit when it reached a slight upgrade. The dealer wouldn't refund his money. Grampa swore he would never buy a used car again but he did buy a used 1926 Dodge truck from a trusted friend. He needed a truck on the farm.

---

[30] Henry Ford made his Model T for the masses and paid his workers well because he wanted them to buy one, but when Ford brought in Frederick Taylor to speed up production at his new River Rouge plant they resisted. Taylor told Ford executives he planned to simplify the workers' tasks so that even a trained chimpanzee (!!) could perform them. When the workers attempted to unionize, the company brought in thugs and the resulting violence and bloodshed soured the labor/management relationship for years.

Ford Motor Company remained nonunion until 1941 when U.S. government applied pressure on both sides to come to terms because American industry was converting to wartime production. Frederick Winslow Taylor is credited today with being the father of scientific management.

By the time the Tirjans settled in Haycock, young Jakie shared driving duty with his father. Blind in one eye from the polio, he could see fairly well in the daylight but not at night; in later life he quit driving altogether. Jakie was glad my father got his license in 1932. Joe could start the car, he could drive the car and he could see where he was going, even after dark.

Despite the car trouble, the Tirjan farm need to take grain to the mill and to bring home supplies. Horses were not reliable. The car was useful for Sunday church and social gatherings but there were so many farm errands that Dad said he rarely got to use the truck for himself. His license to drive was not his ticket to freedom.

He particularly detested delivering milk and eggs in his father's old Dodge truck to prosperous Philadelphia neighborhoods. His customers called him the Farmer Boy. He was NOT a farmer boy. Like his mother, Annie, he missed the city and felt stuck in the country. And he couldn't make a dime because his mother made him turn over every cent he collected as if she thought he was skimming. Even years later Dad became incensed remembering how he worked for no pay and his own mother treated him *like a thief*. He felt she always favored Jakie; his brother got away with everything. In 1934 my father triumphantly bought his own car, a Plymouth bigger than his father's. No more Farmer Boy.

My mother told me she couldn't wait to get off the farm herself. She loved her parents and their Haycock homestead but she and her sister, Cass, envied the modern conveniences other young people enjoyed. Indoor plumbing, for example. It's very cold in Pennsylvania in January and very hot in an outhouse in July. You couldn't invite your friends over to stay. The Haycock house Eva and Cass Schmidt grew up in had no bathroom, no running water—not even cold water—and two outhouses for six people, three of whom were girls blossoming into womanhood. Until eighth grade, the girls rarely got away from farm chores, feeding the livestock, cooking and working in the garden.

As soon as they could find work off the farm, they took jobs as maids in Jewish houses in Philadelphia. They rode the train down from Quakertown on Sunday nights, rented a room and returned home on Fridays. Many people in Haycock commuted like this. Domestic work couldn't have paid them enough to buy a new car, then costing an average of $530, yet somehow they bought one for themselves, a brand new 1931 Plymouth coupe with a rumble seat.

By a great coincidence or perhaps the hand of fate, their father's old friend from Eddystone, a Mr. Jacob Tirjan, had just moved his family to Haycock. He offered to build the girls a proper garage for their car.

Their father knew Jake Tirjan was a good carpenter, and that he, Bruno Schmidt, was not. Thus, a few years before they met Jacob Tirjan Sr.'s sons, the Schmidt sisters future father-in-law built them a fine structure behind their father's barn which would fifteen years later become Smitty's garage.

The sisters went everywhere together. They enjoyed picnics at St. John the Baptist and Saturday night dances at the local Grange Hall but by far the biggest event of the year was the annual Fourth of July carnival at Marienstein Picnic Grounds. Everyone from far and near went to see the fireworks and dance in the pavilion. A local band with a drum, maybe a sax and one accordion—you never need more than one accordion—played pop songs and the old familiar polkas and waltzes. Cass and Eva loved the music they heard on the radio as they cleaned houses in the city. They hadn't bought a radio for their house because Grampa Schmidt would not waste money on the electricity to turn it on.

Eva and Cass' First Car, a 1931 Plymouth with
Rumble Seat

Dad's (Joe Tirjan's) 1934 Plymouth

Eva with 1935 Plymouth in Front of the
Garage Built by Her Future Father-in-Law.
Years Later This Garage Became
Smitty's Workshop

Eva and Joe with 1935 Plymouth
Most Country Roads Were Unpaved

The 1933 Fourth of July was very merry. Prohibition had been repealed so you could buy beer legally for the first time since 1920. In the past, when Eva and Cass went to see the fireworks with their parents they had little spending money, but, grown up now and working, they could afford to buy stylish clothes. On that particular Fourth Cass wore a fancy, new red dress she bought for herself in Philadelphia. Her daughter, Carol Tirjan Muller, still remembers her mother's story about it.

"Dad fell for Mom when he saw that red dress," Carol says. Indeed, Jake Tirjan did fall in love with Cass Schmidt that day.

He bought her a beer. Cass thought he, too, was a sharp dresser, a city slicker. He was witty. They spoke the same language right from the start because his parents were Galizien Deutsche[31] from Königsau, just like hers. When Jake and Cass married in 1935 their younger siblings, Joe Tirjan and Eva Schmidt, were best man and maid-of-honor and presented the newlyweds with a brand new Plymouth as a present.

Joe Tirjan, my father, married Eva Schmidt in June 1936. Since Dad was only twenty, his parents had to sign a legal permission. (Impossible to imagine from my vantage point!) The couple lived in an apartment until Grampa Tirjan offered to carve out a parcel of land for each of his sons to build their own houses. With this generous gift my grandfather set his sons on paths of home building and construction that served them well the rest of their lives.

By the time the United States entered the Second World War, Eva and Joe — and baby Margie — were settled into one of those houses. Jake and Cass and their three babies lived next door in theirs. The nation's mood had improved greatly because big companies such as Bethlehem Steel were hiring again. During the Depression newspapers reported the company had won big contracts such as the Empire State

---

[31] An explanation appears as Appendix I in Philip Semanchuk's, *Just Who Do You Think You Are/Galizien Deutsche.*

Building in 1931, Hoover Dam in 1936 and the Golden Gate Bridge in 1937. But the uptick near the end of the decade wasn't driven by demand for reinforcing rods and girders. The Steel, the name locals called Bethlehem Steel, was the biggest shipbuilder in the country and the munitions business had been very profitable for the company in WWI.[32] Well before hostilities broke out again in Europe in 1939, the company began ramping up production. Employees were discouraged from revealing what they were working on. The warning *Loose Lips Sink Ships* was posted at every worker's station. The wages were good again. The Steel ran buses to pick up workers in outlying areas and many men from Haycock rode a bus to the plant, only fifteen miles away.

In 1939, as the country heaved a sigh of relief that the Depression was finally over, Time magazine named Adolph Hitler Man of the Year. In September German forces invaded Poland and the war in Europe began. On December 7, 1941 Japanese planes bombed the U.S. Fleet in Pearl Harbor and the following day, President Roosevelt declared war on Japan. War with Germany followed soon after.

I was born a few days after the Pearl Harbor attack so I don't recall much about the war except the rationing. Gas was precious: only doctors could get more than one gas ration card because they made house calls. I'm sure the doctor came by on one of those ration cards when I was born in one of those houses Dad and Uncle Jakie built. Sugar and butter were very scarce. Margarine came in a tough plastic bag with a color capsule you burst into the white lard, mixing it through the goop as best you could before you cut the bag open and spread it on toast. Yes, it was a poor substitute for real butter but we had fun squeezing the plastic bag before Mom opened it.

Butter or not, from my earliest days, there was always music on the radio and singing in her kitchen.

---

[32]   From 1910-1914, Bethlehem Steel's average annual earnings were $6,000,000; between 1914-1919 they were $49,000,000.

CHAPTER 11
Ice Cream in December

As early as I can remember I loved going to my Grandma Schmidt's farm in Haycock. On hot summer days I'd explore the pastures and gardens and play in the grassy meadows with her collie, Shep. Then one cold day in December 1945 my mother told me we'd be going to visit her that night. That was strange because this was a trip of ten or eleven miles and we never went there at night in the winter.

Shep and I at Grandma's House
(1950)

The car trip was a special treat in itself because gas had been rationed during the war. Country roads were still very dark at night, not often plowed. I had no inkling why Mom and Dad, Marge, and I would drive out on a snowy night but little boys do not question grown-up plans. We headed down the snow-covered roads, Aunt Cass, Uncle Jake and their kids behind us in their car.

"Mom, I can't see," I whined. It was cold in the back seat but Dad's rule was that kids always sat in the back. Dad's old Plymouth heater had long since quit and he couldn't get parts to fix it during the war.

"Margie, let Jimmy have the middle tonight," Mom said. Margie grumbled. Margie's rule was *not even a finger* over the driveshaft hump, so Mom's permission came as an unusual privilege. Why? I was clueless.

"Ha, ha," I teased from my high point. "I can see right out the windshield and you can't." Big, beautiful snowflakes zoomed into the headlights and disappeared over the car like magic.

Dusty summer roads were now smooth and silent under muffling snow. No cars passed us in either direction. Leaving behind the faint lights of distant houses and dark open fields, the road entered low, marshy woods. Mom wiped fog off the windshield so Dad could see. Marge and I cleared our side windows with our sleeves. But it was dark out beyond the driving snowflakes that began to accumulate along the bottom of the windshield.

We were going to Grandma's! Although Marge was grumpy over on her side, I was happy to be singing Christmas carols. Margie said I was getting too big for my britches but I knew I deserved this treat no matter what the reason. Mom and Dad were cheerful in the front seat, glad to be seeing more of the family but also glad the war was over and the soldiers would be coming home. Dad wouldn't have to be away at the Willow Grove Naval Air Station building military aircraft at Consolidated Vultee, the big defense contractor. And soon, he said, he would be able to buy the spare parts to fix the heater.

We were singing *Jingle Bells* when Uncle Jakie flashed his lights and tooted. We stopped in the middle of nowhere. Without explanation, Dad got out, opened the trunk and disappeared into the darkness with Jakie. We heard loud thuds and smashing sounds like breaking glass, then laughter. Margie and I couldn't see a thing through the swirling snow. Suddenly they reappeared and heaved something heavy into the trunk that made a big thump. Dad brushed snow off the windshield and we set out again. We asked and asked but neither Dad nor Mom would tell us what the men did in the woods or what they put into the trunk. Mom just started to hum *Santa Claus is Coming to Town* and so we all sang along.

The familiar road to Grandma Schmidt's house had become a magical path. The car could be Santa's sleigh, I thought, for nothing looked the same. The huge rock that marked the last leg of our trip to the farm on summer days now loomed like a white wall in the middle of the road, almost invisible.

"Somebody who didn't know it's here would drive right into it tonight," Dad said. "And the rock would win for sure." He inched us around it on the narrow road. "Years ago," he went on, "when the Federal government, the WPA, built this road, the rock was so big they couldn't break it and so heavy they couldn't move it. So they just left it." He sounded pleased that even the Federal government couldn't move Pennsylvania granite.

The road was very dark beyond the headlights because many houses did not yet have electric service. The road didn't even have a name. (In 1961 it was named Harrisburg School Road.) The one-room New Harrisburg Schoolhouse where Mom and the Schmidts went to school stood right across the road from the farm.

When we visited in summer we parked on the side of the road and walked up through Grandma's flower gardens, under a long grape arbor into the sunroom. There would be

Grampa in his rocker reading his German Bible or saying the Rosary. Potted flowers and cactus crowded benches and shelves, filling the porch with blooms and the smells of spring. They never froze because she left the cellar door open, letting warmer air from below rise from bins where she kept root vegetables and the shelves of preserves she had put up the season before.

I made sure never to go anywhere near that cellar because a big black snake lived down there.

"You stay away from him. He's as good as a cat," she warned us kids. "He's there to catch mice. He knows me. I say hello to him every time I go down."

A few years later my cousin, Ed, was surprised by a black snake in the pasture innocently sunning itself on the stone the older boys used for second base. He beat it to death with the bat and when he held it up proudly by the tail, it was as long as he was tall. He ran to show Grandma what he had done.

Oh, she was furious.

"You dumfkopf! Snakes are good!" She grabbed the bloody bat from his hand and flung it as far as she could. Nobody moved a muscle. "You're going to dig me a proper grave for this good old snake, my friend of many years." Her hand on Ed's shoulder, they marched off to the far side of her garden and there was no more baseball for the rest of the day.

That night in December we lugged bags of heavy, drippy stuff in from the trunk, getting snow in our galoshes. A kettle steamed on the stovetop and the aroma of vanilla and butter made my mouth water. We hung a few coats and sweaters on the rickety, old clothes tree near the door and threw the rest on the sofa in the cold living room. For a time in the summer the coatrack had been my secret hiding place where we hung our wet raincoats. I liked to eavesdrop on the grownups although I never understood a word of their

German. When I pulled the whole thing over they laughed to discover me and that was the end of that.

I sniffed. "Do I smell cake?"

"Maybe," Mom said, unloading a heavy, crunchy bag. Dad and Uncle Jakie were making a lot of noise in the sunroom, moving something heavy around. I heard muffled smashing sounds.

"First we're all going to have a special treat." She pushed open the door to the sunroom. "Here's the salt," she called through the doorway.

A big tin washtub now stood in the blooming room, half filled with crushed ice. In the middle of the tub stood a galvanized bucket with a crank handle on one side. Uncle Jakie shook salt from the bag over the ice and then added another layer of ice right up to the rim of the bucket. So that was the mysterious sound, tinkling pieces of breaking ice.

"Jimmy, we have a surprise for you. Peach ice cream," Mom said. "Your favorite. Put your scarf on, it's pretty chilly out here. Grandma's got everything ready."

Grandma poured cream, her canned peaches and some of the precious sugar we had brought. I remembered ice cream from summer when we went to the corner grocery store to get it. I had never heard of anyone making it. Then she set in the wooden paddles. Grampa fitted on the metal top and attached the crank handle. We waited a few minutes for the cold to penetrate the bucket. Grampa laid a hand on it and nodded.

"Now we have to turn the handle to turn the paddles until it gets thick. Then it will harden," Grandma said. "You first, Jimmy," She showed me how to turn it. The older kids watched impatiently.

"He's too little," Margie said.

Grandma glared at her.

"Got enough salt?" Mom asked.

"Took three pounds. That should cool it."

It was hard work. After a dozen turns I was glad to let the others have a chance. By the time it firmed up, no one was asking for a turn.

"That's enough," Grandma said finally. Dad and Uncle Jakie carefully lifted the ice cream bucket out of the ice, set it on the floor and knocked the ice off the sides. Dad shook his fingers and blew on them.

Grandma lifted out the wooden paddles dripping pink ice cream. "This is for the special boy," she said, handing them to me. She tucked a towel around my neck to catch the soft ice cream as it ran down my chin. Margie and my cousins, then everyone dipped their spoons to scoop up what was falling and what lay in peach-flecked swirls below.

Yet it wasn't until they lit four candles on the cake and sang *Happy Birthday* to me that I realized that all this fuss was about me! They hadn't celebrated birthdays during the war and even after, I would never get presents because December 11 was so close to Christmas.

We ate the all the ice cream and scraped the last frosting off the cake plate. I ate so fast I got a headache and a tummy ache. The celebration over, adult conversation drifted away from the subject of wonderful me and my birthday, to the weather, cars, jobs and other boring topics. More and more they spoke German so Grampa could join in. As the ice cream headache faded, my eyelids grew very heavy. I slipped into the living room, closed the door and crawled onto the cushiony sofa under warm wooly coats. The last thing I remember was the murmur of their rising and falling voices in the next room.

This was the best birthday of my entire life.

CHAPTER 12

Musical Maccabees

In the beginning, music came from a white plastic radio in our kitchen and I loved it.

I didn't care for television. Uncle Jakie, who lived right next door, bought a set in 1948 and played it so loudly it kept me awake at night. Dad and his brother loved *The Friday Night Fights*. They hooted and hollered as two grown men in bathing suits, usually two large black men, slugged each other. They bounced up and down on their toes in a square called a ring. Television didn't make much sense to me and the women never watched the Fights, either. The radio was always on and they always sang along.

I was about eight when Mrs. Wrigley, a music teacher in our town, organized a new children's accordion band. I had no interest in joining. To me accordion players were old men in white shirts and red suspenders who played at weddings. I didn't understand the words to their German songs and I didn't like their German music. However, my sister, Margie, and my cousins signed up for the band so I had to, as well. I'll never know why Mrs. Wrigley named the band *The Maccabees,* who were a tribe of courageous Jews whose rebellion is celebrated today by Hanukah. If there was a single Jewish kid in the Maccabees, I didn't know of it. Our costumes made us look more like Spanish cowboys: red satin blouses, black slacks, white sashes and flat-brimmed black flamenco hats trimmed with white ball fringe. Yes, an accordion band.

Maccabees Accordion Band (1950)
I am in the Front Row, Third from the Left
with my Hat Perched on the Back of my Head

We took lessons at Mrs. Wrigley's music store where she sold glockenspiels, drums and, of course, accordions. Squeezing the bellows while fingering the keyboard at the same time was hard. I hated it. I watched the clock every minute of every hour. Mom made sure I practiced every day preparing for the next lesson on every beautiful, wasted Tuesday afternoon. On top of practicing and lessons, we had Saturday morning band practice. After a few months Mrs. Wrigley said we sounded good and we were ready to perform.

At first we marched in Halloween parades on crisp, fall evenings and then right in front of Santa Claus in a cold Thanksgiving Day parade. We played on Memorial Day when other kids were slugging home runs and we roasted in a pavilion on the Fourth of July. We played on old bandstands where there were more mosquitos than audience and on Sunday afternoons in hot, smelly nursing homes in towns like Scranton and Reading after long, stuffy car rides. The audiences, half of them our faithful relatives, applauded enthusiastically. We got our picture in the local newspaper.

Then after one concert, Mrs. Wrigley, always on the lookout for other opportunities to perform, brought us great news: the Maccabees would play on television. In Philadelphia! We'd be contestants on Paul Whiteman's *TV Teen Club*. Paul Whiteman was a famous bandleader at the time, popular with my parents and older kids. I never watched his weekly shows. All I remembered about television was *The Friday Night Fights,* which I didn't like, and westerns and cartoons, which I did.

Early one April Saturday, the Maccabees boarded a nice, big bus but Margie and I had to follow in the car with Mom and Dad, who had volunteered to be chaperones. I had never been to a big city before. We passed through leafy suburbs and began a long descent down Broad Street to the city center. I couldn't believe my eyes. Three rows of cars and buses going in each direction and narrow streets off to the right and left between close, tall buildings. Traffic lights and shops, people walking or standing at the corners, busy in every direction as far as I could see from the back seat. Dad pointed out the distant, tall City Hall building topped with the statue of William Penn. He was the city founder, Dad said, but he was too busy keeping up with the bus to explain what that meant.

Where brick row houses lined city blocks, we saw families just sitting on their front steps, just watching us go by. Dad said the steps were white marble and that the people scrubbed them every Saturday morning. These people had black skin! I had never seen black people before except on *The Friday Night Fights*. But here were black-skinned women and little kids too, just like me. Margie and I discussed this strange phenomenon and begged Dad to slow down so we could look more carefully but he wouldn't.

"Don't stare and do *not* point at them," my mother hissed. "Just look straight ahead!" She didn't explain that, either. I grumbled. What should I look at then, the cloth pattern on the back of Dad's seat? As soon as she faced front again, I did look out the side and she glared at me the way she did when I watched her nursing my baby brother, Fred. How could I *not* watch?

As the traffic slowed and the car got hot, Dad kept that big air-conditioned bus in sight, worried at every stoplight it would get away from us and he wouldn't know where to go. When we finally pulled up to a tall building with the huge letters WFIL on the front, the bus driver was already unloading accordion cases. Margie and I burst out of the car, grabbed our accordions from the trunk and hurried to catch up. At the front of the building, we shuffled through the revolving glass door with our clunky accordion cases jammed between our knees. Inside we seemed to be in a spacious bank lobby; there was even a guard. Mrs. Wrigley stood beside him passing out identification badges so we could use the elevator up to the fourth floor. Only the fourth floor, she cautioned us, nowhere else.

My first ever elevator ride took us up to the television studio, designed like a movie theater but with a stage in front. Big black metal lights hung from wires running across the ceiling and men wore metal earmuffs with dangling wires. There were only six rows of seats set on an arc so each had a full view of the stage. Mrs. Wrigley told us to sit up front. Behind the last row seats hung a wide, tall black curtain, painted with silvery, bubble shapes made to look like more audience heads in more rows. We Maccabees were very interested in that strange curtain and kept turning around to look at it. As we whispered and giggled, a man's voice boomed out from somewhere.

"Keep the noise down and pay attention. Your dress rehearsal is about to begin." Mrs. Wrigley frowned at us as Paul Whiteman strode onto the stage wearing a suit and holding a microphone. He was very large. He explained the rules of the contest to be held at 8:00 that night. There would be three "acts" in the competition. Then he explained how the three cameras worked: the one with the little red light on was the one that was 'live.' If that camera was aimed at you and the red light was on, that's what people saw on their TV sets. The Applause-O-Meter measured how hard the audience clapped so that the act with the loudest applause would be the winner. If we made a mistake in the afternoon rehearsal, he'd give us one chance to do it over. But for the 8:00 PM show, it was once-and-done.

In the rehearsal we played our song perfectly the first time. Mrs. Wrigley smiled. The other contestants, three tap dancers and a singing brother-and-sister act, were pretty good, too. Most of my attention, though, was on the TV cameras, the Applause-O-Meter and those ghostly audience heads on the curtain at the back of the room.

We were free for the rest of the afternoon. One of the chaperones shepherded us out of the studio to Horn and Hardart, an automated cafeteria where you could buy food from tiny boxes with glass doors that opened when you put the right coins in the slot. I bought a hot dog and a piece of lemon meringue pie. Like magic, a black hand in the back replaced the pie as soon as I took mine out.

Then the chaperone took us down long, wide stairs, right under the sidewalk, for a ride on the subway. When the train roared into the station and screeched to a stop, the doors slapped open and crowds of people poured out. Our chaperone hurried us into a car just before the doors closed and told us to hang on as we zoomed down Market Street. Here we got off, walked across the platform and got onto another train that zoomed us back again. When we walked up the stairs, we were right in front of that WFIL building. I couldn't believe it. Hundreds of people rode the subway in both directions, all the time, right there under the sidewalk.

Inside the building there were surprises too. When we rode up and down on the elevators—which we knew we weren't supposed to do—numbers lit up over the doors. People got on and off. Cousin Mike hadn't gone with us for the subway ride. He'd stayed behind to explore the building and when I got back he had something to show me but only if I could keep a secret. Of course I could.

The fifth floor elevator door opened onto a big room decorated something like a circus or a carnival. Several tall, wide, colorful curtains hung from the ceiling, like the one with the silvery audience heads. On one curtain a painted boat sailed a painted sea. On another, painted lights shone on a painted city street. On a third, painted cactus and rocks showed a painted desert scene just like those in TV westerns.

On the other side of the room, a life-sized stuffed horse on wheels, saddled and ready to ride, waited patiently among Roman columns and statues. Boxes, ladders, all kinds of stuff, too much to take in, crowded the floor. It was very quiet and dark in the corners. I was sure we were not supposed to be there.

Mike grabbed my arm. "Over here. You gotta see this."

Behind the horse, shoved into a dim corner, three life-sized, bare-breasted, golden mermaids offered clusters of grapes from a dry fountain. I stared. Fake mermaid with fake breasts—TV used a lot of stuff to fool people, the same way carnival magicians did. I still liked radio better.

At exactly eight PM we were up first and performed "*Oh, Dem Golden Slippers*," an old Negro spiritual, long a Philadelphia favorite. The other two acts went up; we could see the tap dancers were very good. The Applause-O-Meter agreed. They won and we came in second. The singing brother and sister finished last and burst into tears.

We never did see ourselves on television because TV shows were transmitted live in those days. If it had been recorded, I might have watched. But probably not.

The Maccabees never performed on TV again and I could finally quit the accordion. The subway remains my favorite part of the adventure.

That Market Street studio was the first one in the country designed specifically for television broadcasting. Owner Walter Annenberg brought in Dick Clark, a young radio DJ from Utica, New York to clean up a problem with one TV program. Clark's predecessor, Bob Horn, was fixing up young girls on his *Bandstand* show to meet older men who were interested in more than their dance steps. But Clark was squeaky-clean and the scandal soon faded into history. The ABC-TV network picked up Clark's *American Bandstand* show and broadcast from that same Philadelphia studio until it moved to Hollywood in 1964.

Today's Annenberg Schools of Communication at USC and the University of Pennsylvania trace some of their roots to that building on 46th and Market with revolving glass doors and subway trains zooming past just beneath the sidewalk. Unfortunately, all that remains of the station today is WFIL-AM, a Christian teaching and talk radio station.

CHAPTER **13**

The Suitcase

Childhood is a dream from which we wake slowly into the adult world and its cares and troubles. One day we notice that adults have personalities that exist separate from us children. On one Sunday when we didn't go to Mass, Margie and I witnessed conflict in the grown-up world we took for granted. In my mind's eye I recall that bewildering morning.

No church today? Margie and I sat in the back seat, straining to hear what Dad and Mom were talking about. He drove us off fast and turned onto the long dirt road to the house Dad and Uncle Jakie had built for their parents, an unadorned little box in an empty landscape. No trees, no lawn, no neighbors.

"She's lonesome, Eva," Dad said. They were arguing about Grandma Tirjan. Dad always stuck up for her, although everybody knew she favored Jakie because he was her first and he had that polio.

"She hasn't done much to make any friends at church." Mom sighed impatiently. "She's . . . I don't know, she's different." We knew Grandma Tirjan's disparaging remarks about Quakertown irritated Mom. The more Grandma complained about the town—and the isolated countryside she was living in—the more Mom stuck up for it. She said she would never leave Quakertown and she never did.

"She can go back to Eddystone as far as I'm concerned," Mom added. Dad's shoulders lifted and fell.

Margie and I had similar opinions about Grandma Tirjan. First, we weren't sure she even liked us. Sometimes she sighed when she looked out the window at the pastures surrounding the house, talking to herself in German. Grownups could talk about anything in that language knowing we wouldn't understand. This made us feel we had done something wrong, that we should be more careful, that we weren't good grandchildren.

Dad pulled into the gravel driveway next to the farmhouse, got out and slammed his door before I could push his seat forward to climb out.

"You kids stay out here," he called over his shoulder as he hurried up the porch steps and went inside.

"Did somebody die?" Margie asked. Dad never hurried like that.

"Stay here. We'll be back in a few minutes."

"Why can't we come in too?" I whined.

"Because you can't. Not now." Mom closed her door firmly and went up the steps, carrying the last of our breakfast strudel. We always took something good to eat when we visited Grandparents.

"I'm hungry," I said.

"Don't," Margie said. We stared at the house, willing the door open.

"Somebody *is* sick and they aren't telling us."

I sat back and put my feet up on the front seatback. Margie pushed them off. I rolled my window up and down, up and down. The old car didn't have a clock but time seemed to stretch for an hour. There was nothing to look at outside: the house, the little concrete block barn next to it, too new to offer any adventures.

No cars went by on the road below us because there were no other houses on the road. The sky was perfectly blue, not a cloud in sight to announce any change in the weather. There weren't any cows in the fields. Chickens wandered in the pen attached to the barn and we knew the pig would be sleeping on the far side. Sometimes we took stale bread to them but we had left the house so fast that morning there was no time to gather leftovers. If you didn't feed the pig he would just lie in the mud flicking flies off his ears.

We crawled into the front seats and polished the dashboard dials with our sleeves. We didn't touch the keys that hung in the ignition but the thought occurred to both of us. If we could drive, where would we go?

"I wish we'd gone to church today," I said. If we were in church the service would be almost over. There you could at least look at other people and hear the organ music. We didn't sing at Mass but there was a choir in the back and you could tell when the service was almost over because the music got louder. After Mass we would go to Gugliangelos Grocery for fresh bread and sliced ham, our usual Sunday lunch. I could hear Margie's stomach rumble.

We were so well-behaved it never occurred to us to get out of the car. Our parents trusted us to stay put. They would not forget us. They would look out the window and wave to us, soon. But they didn't.

"Maybe Mom's letting Grandma have it for being mean to us," I said. Now we could hear Dad and Grandma and then Grampa arguing loudly in the front room.

"Yeah. Mom was really mad. But that was way last summer." Margie said thoughtfully. She cocked her head to hear the sounds from the house. "What's that?"

A curtain twitched at the window but fell back again.

"Grandma's grouchy." I was feeling grouchy myself. "Why doesn't she just go back there to the city?"

We gazed at the empty fields. Even if we got out of the car there'd be no place to go. That was the problem when we came to stay that night with Grandma last summer.

I was eight when Margie and I stayed at Grandma Tirjan's. Neither of us wanted to go but Mom said we had to, that Grandma Tirjan would think we loved Grandma Schmidt more than her if we didn't. So Dad and Mom drove us over. When we walked into the kitchen, it smelled like pie.

Grandma's face lit up to see Dad. They hugged and she offered them coffee. They thanked her but said they had to go, reminded us to behave ourselves and left.

"You can put your things down right here," Grandma said, wiping her hands on a dishtowel and eyeing us. "I see you've both grown. Let's measure." I backed up to the doorframe where all our heights and years were recorded.

"An inch and a half since you've been here," she exclaimed. "It's not like I live so far away."

The afternoon passed without any incidents—I don't remember what we did. Not much. Supper at five and then straight to bed for us.

"It's too early," I complained. "The sun's still up. I want to go outside and play." The house was hot.

"I don't care about the sun. It's bedtime."

Margie stayed on the porch, smacking mosquitos, ignoring Grandma.

"I'm not going if Margie doesn't go." We weren't babies. We always stayed up until dark.

"Grampa? The kids won't go to bed." When she set her mouth in a line I felt I didn't really know this lady in an old housedress.

Grampa sighed. "Come on, kids. You'll be asleep soon and forget about this tomorrow."

"I want to go home," I whimpered. Margie and I dutifully lay down on the rollout sofa and waited for the day to end. A metal strap poked our backs. The house was tiny. Grandma and Grampa slept in a small bedroom right off the kitchen. They soon fell asleep and snored. Margie and I tried not to talk or laugh or punch each other but we had never slept in the same room together, let alone in the same bed. We were really restless.

"Quiet down," Grandma said, the first time she woke up. But one of us would think of something funny, her German words, her dress, the way her hair fell down her neck, her missing tooth. We couldn't stop giggling.

"You make me do this," Grandma growled as she reached for the phone. "Eva? They're too much for me. They won't go to sleep." Pause. "Danke."

She turned to us. "They'll be here to get you soon so get dressed and gather up your things. Don't leave anything behind."

Judging from my mother's face when she arrived, her curt thank you and the way she hustled us into the car, Mom and Dad had been looking forward to an evening alone. Margie and I didn't care. We wanted to go home.

"Did you have fun?" Mom mechanically asked from the front seat.

"Sort of." Margie said. "She doesn't have a radio."

"She has a radio," I corrected. "But she won't turn it on because she doesn't like the stations."

"She made us go to bed way early."

"As if we were bad. And it was so hot. She wouldn't open even one window."

"That's it," Mom said to Dad who was looking straight ahead. "I've tried. Let her other grandchildren stay there."

"Oh, Eva. She's lonesome."

The hot car smelled of engine oil and dusty upholstery. The strudel would be completely gone by now. I should have had seconds at breakfast. Just then Uncle Jakie and Aunt Cass pulled in.

"Hello," we called, hoping they would liberate us, but they walked right past without even looking, up the steps and inside. We heard sounds of angry protests and accusations, all in German. We had never heard anyone argue like that. Maybe they really were fighting. Then the front door banged open and Grandma stormed out wearing her coat and gloves and carrying a suitcase. She paused, shouted something in German, then clomped down the steps banging the suitcase behind her. Dad, Mom, Uncle Jakie, Aunt Cass and Grampa filed out and watched, red-faced. Mom and Cass dabbed their cheeks. Where did she get a suitcase, we wondered. She dragged it to Uncle Jakie's car and stood by the passenger door like someone waiting for a ride. She was only a few feet away from us.

"Mom, don't do this," Uncle Jakie said. "Come back into the house now. Let's talk."

"I'm done talking. I hate this house, I hate this country and I wish I could go home," she said. "Take me away. Anywhere. I'll get a bus." Her voice broke.

"Now, come on. What'll Pop do?" Jakie reached for her. "He can't live alone."

"I want to live with my own people!" She stepped away from him in a sudden fury. "I never wanted to come so far from home. Nothing but chickens and Mennonites. Now you move away to the other side of town. And don't think I don't know your father gave you money for that new place."

"Oh, Mom, it's a loan, a business deal."

She had turned to look down the empty road.

"We built you this nice house and Betty's only two miles away. We're not far either." He didn't move to the driver's side and, for a long moment, no one else moved. When Grandma realized that neither Jakie nor Dad would take her away, she flung the suitcase away and slumped against the car, sobbing. We could see the keys hanging from the ignition in plain sight right in front of her. For forty years she had refused to learn to drive.

"Jake, take her to Betty's," Dad said, finally. He put her suitcase in the back seat.

That was the Sunday with no church and grownups who acted in very disturbing ways and, even worse, seemed not to have noticed us at all. Grampa finally bought a house in Quakertown and she moved back in. It wasn't Eddystone but there were sidewalks and neighbors she could talk to.

I think Grandma's homesickness explained her gloomy nature. Perhaps she never settled into a neighborhood. Perhaps that was why she invited those boring, German-speaking cronies from the city up to her holiday dinners. They reminded her of happier times. Margie and I never talked about this. Now I know we could have been kinder.

Chapter 14

A Free Man

"When I was your age, my mother made me a *milkman* selling eggs and cheese to rich people," Dad reminded me. "Hard work never hurt anybody. You're lucky to even get this job. Make the most of it; maybe you'll learn something. Since you no longer have a car you can darn well stay down there with Jake and Cass."

I had got into trouble almost as soon I started work at the county farm at Neshaminy Manor Home that my Uncle Jakie, now Uncle Jake, was bossing. One night in June, after a long day in the fields, I drove home as usual, cleaned up, took a girl to my last high school prom and drove her home. Then I went looking for a party with my friend, Tom.

I was tired but we really wanted to make that party. If I got sleepy, an unlikely circumstance since I was the invincible age of seventeen, my head would drop onto the steering wheel and blow the car horn to wake me up. But at four in the morning, as the eastern sky was brightening, I nodded off and hit a telephone pole, hard. My head went right through the steering wheel and the horn blew until the police disconnected it. Tom and I went to the hospital where I lay in a coma for five days.

Mom and Dad were scared—and furious at my poor judgment: I could have killed Tom and myself. They had the bills for the car, a new telephone pole and my hospital stay. Our insurance rates went up. Then Tom's parents sued.

"What were you thinking?" Mom asked. "We thought you had more sense."

Dad was disgusted. I couldn't do one thing right: when Mom came to pick me up at the hospital, I ran down the back stairs to meet her as she took the elevator up to the third floor. My empty room, curtains blowing out the open window, scared the hell out of her.

I had completely disgraced myself.

Summer in southeastern Pennsylvania is as hot and humid as anywhere in the country. By late June, the waist-high string beans had grown so thick we had to fight our way down the rows. Because crops grow like crazy in such weather, the beans were ready to harvest. If they weren't picked before the Fourth, they'd be too far-gone even for canning. But the rows of beans stretched for a thousand yards — half a mile — from the County buildings straight down to a drop off to heavy traffic on Route 611, the main highway between Doylestown and Philadelphia. No matter how fast we worked, it didn't look like we could bring the crop in on time.

We were laboring at our impossible task when we heard a change in the pitch of traffic noise on the highway. It sounded like a truck had turned into Manor Lane. It ground its gears and groaned slowly up the hill. When it appeared, we saw it was some kind of an old school bus, only grey with barred windows. We heaved a sigh of relief: here were migrant workers to help. In those days, as now, farmers hired crews of professional pickers, migrant labor, often Southern blacks, who followed the harvest from south to north. Now we had a chance to get the beans in by the Fourth and we'd be off for the three-day weekend.

The bus pulled into the shade of a big tree next to the hospital building but the doors remained closed. Then a white cruiser with the bold lettering of the Bucks County Sheriff's Department rumbled up and parked beside it. My heart stopped for a moment, remembering how the police questioned me three times about the night I drove my car into that telephone pole. I couldn't remember anything about it when I came out of the coma five days later. While I knew for sure I hadn't been drinking that night, I'm not sure they believed me.

Then there was that speeding ticket when I lost my license for a few months and had to go into the police station for a stern lecture from the Chief. I'd never seen a Sheriff's cruiser before but it looked an awful lot like a police car.

When John, the farm manager, walked over to the Sheriff's car and spoke a few words in through the window, my heart raced even faster. But they never looked my way. The driver, tall and lean in his uniform and flat-brimmed trooper's hat, got out and shook John's hand. A portly man then struggled out of the passenger door holding a wide-brimmed straw hat and what looked like a shotgun.

The trooper knocked on the bus door. When it opened he leaned in, said something and stepped back to let out the passengers. But these weren't black migrant workers with their lunch sacks, always talking and joking with each other. These were white men in grey pants and long-sleeved blue shirts — inmates from the County Correctional Facility. They crowded together like sheep in a pen, looking nervously around. Farmer John led them to the field in a single file and started them, one at a time, down the rows beside us. So, the prisoners were going to pick beans right next to us. A low hum of protest rumbled among us college boys. They might be no good as pickers and we'd have to do their work over. And now it would be an even longer wait at the water spigot.

Were these men murderers? Probably not, but they could be robbers who stuck up liquor stores or worse. They didn't look around at us or make a sign of any kind to each other. The Sheriff stood off to one side as the fat guard with the gun brought up the rear. Two prisoners lugged a big water can between them and a third carried an old aluminum lawn chair.

The guard set up his lawn chair in the shade of a high tree so he could watch the entire field. He eased his bulk into the chair, adjusted his silvered sunglasses, pulled the brim of his straw hat down to shade his face. He carefully laid the shotgun across his fat thighs. It was a real shotgun. Maybe the Sheriff hadn't come for me this time but this was a real guard watching real inmates picking beans right next to me. We were all within range of that shotgun.

So this was a criminal's life. While our crew could use the bathroom and get a drink of water whenever we wanted, the prisoners had to wait until the whistle blew, then line up at the ends of their rows, file into the bathroom and only then go to their water can. Back to their rows, single file, quickstep, the guard's face turning left and right to scan the fields.

One of the prisoners, obviously an expert picker, was soon only ten feet behind me in the next row.

"Hey there, boy," he said, pleasantly in a soft, Southern drawl. My shirt was soaked and sweat dripped from my nose. "Got a cigarette?"

I shook my head impatiently.

"What's your name?"

I didn't want to talk to this criminal person. And I certainly didn't want the guard seeing me talking to him, so I didn't answer. No one had warned us we'd be working with convicts. I wondered what my mother would think—although I could hear my father saying I deserved this.

But the guy persisted. "Aw, come on, I ain't gonna bite ya."

"Jim," I finally said, without looking at him. He didn't sound like he would bite me. Not at all. Out of the corner of my eye I could see he looked like an ordinary guy wearing prison clothes. With an eye on the guard with the shotgun, I ignored him again.

"Jim, you live on this here farm?" His voice was pleasant. No urgency.

"Nope."

"Where'd ya live then?"

"Twenty miles from here," I said, finally, out of the corner of my mouth. Irritated, but I have to admit, a little bit interested. I wondered what crime the guy had committed but I wasn't about to ask.

"Why're you pickin'? You do something wrong?"

"It's my summer job," I snorted.

"Ain't you lucky, huh?" He grunted noncommittally. Now he was almost beside me. There were only a few beans in his basket. We worked side by side for several minutes. Cicadas hummed and grasshoppers jumped. Bean leaves had stuck to every inch of my skin and clothes and my hands were furry. His, too. He examined his hands and then he spoke again.

"How'd you get this swell job working like a nigger here in the hot sun?"

I stood up to see if John was coming to call us to lunch. No sign of him.

"Uncle runs the place," I sighed.

"He workin' you hard, Mr. Jim. I'm Billy Joe from Ali-bema. Pleased ta meet-cha."

He started to extend his hand but quickly withdrew it. The guard seemed not to have noticed so we fell back to picking. I felt a little easier. True, I was working hard but I could easily see I had picked a heck of a lot more beans than he had.

"How'd you get this?" I asked, glancing at his uniform.

"My woman left me and came north. I followed her, got drunk, beat somebody up and next thing I'm in jail in Doylestown, wherever that is. A few days. I usually work it off."

Usually work it off. It seemed jail was normal for him.

Down on the highway a truck sounded a long blast on its air horn. Billy Joe lifted his head.

"Which way that go?" he smiled. When I saw his broken tooth my tongue ran over my own capped teeth, another expense for my parents who never wanted me to play football in the first place. A gust of self-pity blew over me: was I already as ruined as this skinny, half-shaved prisoner? He spit a glob of bean fuzz to one side as if he were spitting tobacco and looked down toward the busy highway below us.

Billy Joe seemed only a few years older than I but he looked nothing like the college-boy crew with our straight teeth, good haircuts and clean jeans. We would go home to parents who would never let us hang around a burger joint drinking long necks and knocking over little shops for cigarette and beer money. Billie Joe was the kind of guy who got girls in trouble and got himself onto county prison rolls. The kind our parents warned us about.

The highway led back up to Doylestown or down to the city of Philadelphia. I could send him back to Doylestown.

Billy Joe waited.

"Philly," I said, nodding toward the south.

As our crew headed into lunch, the guard asked the way to the kitchen, in a building out of sight beyond the rise where he'd perched his chair. When we had finished our lunch and told him the wash-up and serving procedures, he blew his whistle, barked a command and with his shotgun waved his prisoners across the wide, green lawns.

In twenty minutes or so he hurried them back, yelling and shouting at both them and us. We were too far away in the field to hear what he wanted. Kenny, one of the college boys, moved a little closer to hear, then turned and yelled down to me.

"Jim, you seen Duane? He didn't show up for lunch."

"Who's Duane?" I shouted back.

"That guy working right there next to you."

"You mean . . . ?" I didn't see any Duane or Billy Joe, either. Dammit, it wasn't my job to keep track of a county prisoner. I crushed a big horsefly on my arm and pushed through the bushes into his row. There was his nearly empty basket and a few scuffs in the dirt—what a man crawling on his elbows would make if he were slithering down to the highway to freedom.

I served out the rest of my summer sentence at the Farm. As far as I know, neither one of us ever went back.

CHAPTER 15

Good Friends, Displaced People

When I asked my father why his parents had accents, he testily replied, "We're all immigrants!"[33] End of discussion.

There were plenty of reasons to let the immigration part of the family fade into history. Their old country was the enemy in two world wars and lost both. German-speaking or other foreign-sounding immigrants aroused nativist suspicions of disloyalty. Even if he had even wanted to talk about it, my father could not have found Königsau on a map. Austrians, Germans, Poles and Ukrainians had all taken turns ruling Galicia, changing town names, languages and residents.

Some immigrants came as slaves, indentured servants, political or religious refugees, others to avoid military service or forced labor in their home countries but they all brought their dreams of prosperity to America. Without good English skills, however, assimilation into the English-speaking population was slow. In densely populated areas such as Eddystone where everyone had to learn English to work, shop and go to school, immigrants needed only one generation to blend in. But in many rural areas in

---

[33] He was right. In the 2010 there were 5.2 million Native Americans, about half of whom were of mixed race. The rest of the 309 million Americans either came from somewhere else or their ancestors did.

Pennsylvania immigrants settled near others with the same language, religion and culture for mutual aid and safety. They were suspicious of outsiders and held their families close the way the elder Tirjans and Schmidts did.

In small towns like Haycock and Quakertown we children of old-world families learned to get along in high school. I met Andris Klaupiks in 1952 when we started seventh grade together. Six months older than I, Andy had been born in Riga, Latvia. His family fled as the Soviet Red Army was re-capturing the country from the Germans.[34] I understood nothing about that but I was envious that Andy lived in Applebachsville, a village with a lot of other Latvian children. I had loved it when my family lived briefly in Milford Square because there were many kids to hang out with. Then Dad sold that house and we moved into yet another construction project far from town, where I was bored stiff and got into trouble with the neighborhood toughs. Making friends in high school probably saved me from juvenile delinquency.

Andy and I first met up at a high school basketball game. Coming from the sticks, I didn't know anything about sports but he did. He had learned all the rules and plays and important strategies from older Latvian kids. We went to all the basketball games. Andy would point out what to watch for, how the rules worked, how the momentum shifted back and forth. Not a player but a good writer, he was so knowledgeable he wrote sports reports for the Quakertown Free Press.

Andy had me keep track of fouls, individual scoring, team penalties and so forth—an excellent way to learn the sport. Even though we lived on opposite sides of town we each rode the bus to school, had some of the same classes,

---

[34] In 1939 the Soviets invaded Latvia. In 1941 the Germans drove the Soviets out and occupied the country until 1944 when the Soviets returned and pushed the Germans back out.

played football and ran track together. We were best friends until tenth grade, when he began to carry Tracy Haas' books.

Tracy was smart, bold and really easy to look at. When she sat up straight in class, all the boys noticed. And for a long time, Andy seemed to be her favorite guy. Tracy was proud that she was Jewish, a very small minority in our town. She was articulate and had strong opinions about world affairs, Zionism and social issues we never thought about. She was a presence in all her classes and she was very pretty. Andy was good-looking, too. They made a handsome couple.

I went to school dances and other dances in town, where the music was lively and kind of sexy, especially at the West End Fire House where we put down our really good moves, more than we could do at high school sock hops. Aside from that, because I was the youngest kid in my class, by the time I got my driver's license most guys already had cars and steady girlfriends. Although Tracy and Andy walked the school corridors together and she went out with him, she invited other boys and girls to her parties and sometimes included me.

Once at a party at Tracy's house with about a dozen classmates I saw no sign of Andy. Whether they were on the outs or he had a story to file, I was just happy to be included. Apart from these few opportunities to mingle, I never thought much about her. I was clueless about girls but I knew she was too sophisticated for a boy like me.

I felt a little scared about graduation. As the time drew near, I felt I was behind in everything: love, for one thing because I hadn't gone to enough parties with girls, and French, because I hadn't studied enough for the final exam.

One happy day as she sat beside me in French class, Tracy asked if I was prepared for the exam the next day.

I half shrugged. I was never prepared enough.

"I find French hard, too," she said with a smile. "Why don't you come over tonight and we'll review everything? There's a lot to cover. We'll work on what we don't know."

"OK." Wow.

My father noticed as I tried to slip out the door.

"Hey, don't you have to study tonight? You're not finished with your finals are you?"

I was ready.

"That's the problem, Dad. The French final's tomorrow. It's hard studying that stuff by myself." Mom and Dad never forgave me for taking French instead of German. They could have helped me with German. But German was for scientists. The language of diplomacy was French, school advisors had told us, and that sounded pretty good to me.

"So, Tracy's invited some of us over. Apparently everybody's having problems."

"Where are you going?" my mother asked, distractedly.

"To Tracy's. Tracy Haas. She's a brain and even she's worried."

My father said, "Haas? Is that Herb Haas' daughter. The Jew that owns the shoe store?"

"Yes. Tracy." I slid out the door. "She's really nice. See ya later."

As I pressed the Haas' doorbell, I noticed the brass Mezuzah on the jamb. When Tracy asked me in, I saw there was no sign of her parents, not even a faint aroma of the night's dinner in the air. Perhaps they were upstairs or out on business. I expected a group study session, yet I was only person there.

"Why don't we go back to the reading room?"

Tracy's reading room! I had heard discrete talk about this 'reading room'. College-bound guys in our class spoke of it almost with awe. These guys were not lustful, brutish braggarts but seriously smart. The reading room was a great privilege.

Yet. When she closed the door behind me, I asked if anyone else was coming. No, she said, it's just the two of us. So I shrugged and opened my book.

"Let's start with the hard parts," she suggested.

"Well, I'm having a tough time with verb tenses and moods." I flipped through the pages.

"Come sit right next to me so I can see your notes." She patted the sofa cushion beside her.

Whew! I fanned through the lessons, trying to concentrate, looking for the troublesome 'mood verbs' like 'wished for' or 'need'. Sweating a little, I looked up to see her smiling face. Her upright posture made the front of her sweater very obvious. Uh oh. At this rate we might not get any studying done. We were mere inches apart.

"Oh, Tracy," I said. What was the polite thing to say now? Was this some kind of an invitation? "I don't think . . . If I fail tomorrow I won't get into college."

I was in way over my head here. Sensing my panic, she backed off as I closed my book and stood up.

"OK, go home then," she said crisply, then more softly. "But it's still early. We have time before tomorrow morning."

Then her mood shifted again.

"But if you want to leave, just go right ahead."

I had pissed her off. In agonized confusion I sat stupidly in my car. What an idiot I was to walk out on the Great Tracy Haas after all the years of watching her from afar. My one chance. Should I go back in? Dumb idea. She wouldn't ever let me back in.

And if she did, I'd never study and I'd flunk the final and never get to college and spend the rest of my life in Quakertown. Oh man, why tonight?

Alone in my room, I couldn't concentrate on French verbs or anything but my clumsy behavior. But it didn't matter because the final was a snap and I've never spoken a word of French since. However, I have always wondered if I would have kissed her if she weren't Andy's girlfriend. If she hadn't been Jewish. I blew it and have regretted it ever since.

I went to the Senior Prom with another girl and wrecked my car. Many people sent me flowers and cards in the hospital but the one from Tracy signed Love was the one I still remember. She wrote that she was moving away and wished me well. I had no car and worked at the farm twenty miles away so I missed all the post-graduation parties where I might have seen her again.

That fall she left for college in Boston, Andy left for Duke and I headed up to Lehigh. I stayed in touch with Andy; he was a writer and I was a business major. We boys had always drunk beer in high school but Andy drank more than any of us. Now he was way down in North Carolina. I could see we were going our separate ways.

The next summer I got a job working construction while Andy worked in Brooklyn as a hospital orderly with our other good friend, Tom. Once again I was envious of Andy. While I rode back-and-forth to work with my father, learned the carpenter trade, joined a union and earned better money than he and Tom, they were out on their own a mere subway ride from New York City.

I was a junior at Lehigh two years later when I saw Tracy again at a party in Quakertown. She had dropped out of college her freshman year because it was too 'cliquish'. Perhaps being Jewish was a factor in her feeling excluded; maybe coming from a small town was worse. She had moved to London and married the Brit she introduced. He spoke with such a strong accent none of us locals could understand him and, of course, we all gave him the cold shoulder. Tracy had picked up a British accent of her own in those two years. Assimilation, again. I tried to imagine how wonderful it would be to be out on the town in London with this exotic bird—but I would never know.

CHAPTER 16

Driving to Cuba

"Are you sure you don't want Dad and me to take you to college?" Mom asked me, at least three times. "We'd be happy to!"

"No thanks," I replied breezily. "I'll go up with Eddie's folks." Eddie was a high school classmate also enrolled as a Lehigh freshman.

Were they disappointed not to take their number one son to his college dorm? I was the first in the family to go past high school. Because I was living twenty miles away at the county farm, I hadn't seen the orientation package Lehigh had sent to my house. When Eddie's folks dropped me at my dorm building, I saw my new classmates touring the campus with their proud, happy families and realized my mistake. My heart sank. The building was so empty and quiet I really missed them and home seemed very far away.

Then I heard voices down the hall. A suitcase propped the door open so I knocked.

"Come right in!" answered a young voice in perfect English. There were three Cubans, Rolando, George and Roberto, in my class. They were even further from home and they didn't come with their parents. I felt a little better. And I was thrilled to meet actual foreign guys. All I knew about Cuba I learned in Current Events—Fidel Castro had overthrown the Bautista government—and from watching *I Love Lucy*.

While I was thrilled to meet them, they were disappointed that there were no girls on campus, that we had Saturday morning classes and that the legal drinking age was twenty-one so the bars in South Bethlehem were off limits. The exotic lives of these three made mine feel small. I longed to see that bigger world.

When I got back to school in January for second semester, I was surprised to find the Cubans already there. Nobody cuts vacation time short. Their parents sent them out of Cuba early, fearing they could be trapped by a Castro travel ban. On a mission to cleanse Cuba of the Mafia and corrupt foreign businesses, Fidel Castro had immediately closed the casinos, then seized the assets of General Electric, General Motors and Coca Cola. Roberto's family had been part of Bacardi for generations. Rolando's family had financial interests on the island too. This was very heady stuff for a Quakertown boy. As they talked politics, I happily lit up a cigar and drank a glass of the rum they had brought back. Life must be good in Havana.

George disagreed with Rolando's point of view. Bautista was not only corrupt, he was cruel. He had treated Cubans like slaves. The new Castro government would change everything for the better, he insisted. The country was only ninety miles from Miami; why didn't Americans know anything about this? Whenever I began to make sense of it, George's passionate diatribes slid into Spanish and I couldn't tell if I agreed with him. Rolando and Roberto, completely opposed to what they saw as the destruction of their of life, let George rant on, only occasionally interrupting to sharply disagree.

In the second semester, Rolando, Roberto and I joined Phi Kappa Theta, a Catholic fraternity. Jewish George wouldn't join any fraternity that would have him, although there were Jewish frat houses. That spring there were many long-distance toll calls on our fraternity house phone to Miami and Havana. The Cubans always paid for them. I never called Quakertown; it was too expensive.

In September 1960, my sophomore year, Rolando and Roberto returned from Cuba with stories of the great summer they spent at their families' beach houses with girlfriends. No jobs for them. My worldly status had improved from farm laborer to construction laborer. I could only dream of their lives in that island paradise.

In October, the Pirates beat the Yankees 10-9 in the seventh game of the World Series on Bill Mazeroski's home run. We went wild. In November Kennedy beat Nixon, in December, the Eagles beat the Green Bay Packers, and we celebrated both times. The music was great: Fats Domino and Peter, Paul and Mary played the Lehigh campus. Then came the season of 1960-1961, a season of particularly nasty weather in the northeast.

Bethlehem, Pennsylvania, was a gloomy steel company town in those days. A smoky pall of hydrogen sulfide from the steel furnaces hung in the air the winter *Where the Girls Are,* a movie about four coeds on spring break in Ft. Lauderdale, opened in town. This had to be the greatest Florida promotion ever produced: gorgeous young girls in bathing suits lounged on sunny beaches sipping coconut drinks. Florida looked even better than Cuba. As Hank, André and I, fraternity brothers, walked out of the theater into the grim weather, we immediately agreed to drive down to Ft Lauderdale right after our January finals in my old car. We could lie on the beach and live it up just like in the movie. When Rolando heard about our plans he asked to come along. Then George and Roberto wanted in. The Cubans didn't drive but they'd pay their share, so we said sure.

This would be my first real trip to Florida. Those trips with my parents when I was just a kid in the back seat didn't count. I never considered whether my '55 Chevy would take six of us thirteen hundred miles to Florida and thirteen hundred back. I would have gone anyway.

We headed out of Bethlehem one grey January morning, three in front and three sleeping Cubans in the back, as storm warnings interrupted the radio music. We paid no attention. The weather had nothing to do with us. Yet the clouds grew darker as we pushed through downtown traffic in Philadelphia, then Wilmington, Baltimore and Washington.

The engine labored under the load; then sleet bounced off the windshield. Snow-blurred headlights blinded us and we could barely see the red taillights in front of us in the long lines of city traffic. We started to pick up speed again just outside of Richmond when the rear tire blew. We emptied our summer clothes out of the trunk, found the old spare and both parts of the jack, loosened the too-tight lug nuts and changed the steaming tire. We loaded everything back in, found a garage, put the fixed tire put back on, reloaded the trunk and set off again. Somewhere in North Carolina, another tire blew. It was very quiet inside the car now. When the third tire blew in Georgia I wondered, for the first time, if we would make it.

When we crossed the Florida state line it was another 365 miles to Miami, where we would drop off the Cubans. This had seemed an insignificant distance on a map when we were in Bethlehem but after thirty-six hours on the road it was torture. They woke up as we pulled into Little Havana after midnight. The streets were alive with a market and music. Rolando's relatives welcomed us with hugs but did not offer us any place to sleep. A little dismayed, we agreed to pick them up in a week and watched wistfully as they disappeared into the happy throng.

But palm trees rattled in the warm tropic air, just as we had imagined. A pal of Hank's let us sleep on his dorm room floor for two nights and it felt great to be part of the cheering crowd at my first big college basketball game. Determined to make the most of our Miami time, we headed out to Miami Beach, *Where the Girls Are*. On either side of the long causeway from the mainland, lights gleamed on the water when three beautiful girls in a convertible pulled alongside.

"Ella Fitzgerald's at the Eden Roc," they called. "Follow us!"

This was the moment that made the storm, the flats, the long hours crammed into my car worth every minute. The movie hadn't lied. We dug into our pockets and added up our cash.

Alas! We hadn't counted on spending so much money on the way down: the new, second-hand tire and several quarts of oil, not to mention more gas than we expected. So now we were just about broke and we couldn't afford Ella Fitzgerald at the Eden Roc. I'll never forget the sight of those dreamlike young women as they vanished into the night traffic. We turned back and headed north to Lauderdale.

We arrived in Lauderdale and right into the teeth of the storm that had chased us all the way from Pennsylvania. We froze in our tee shirts. I climbed one palm tree but it was too cold to swim and when we lay on the beach the wind sandblasted us. Our motel room was cheap—because there were no tourists. We looked into a few bars where some pale-white guys stood around in ski jackets, but we couldn't afford a 'Cuba Libre', rum and Coke, or even a plain Coke. We would have gone home right then but we dutifully waited until we could go back to Miami to pick up the Cubans before heading north.

No sleeping in the back seat this time. The Cubans were full of lively talk, all in Spanish, very excited about seeing their families again. We agreed we all had a great time even if we didn't have a tan to show for it. We got back to Lehigh just in time to register for second semester.

The next day the Cubans were gone. They packed up and left Lehigh without a word. We were shocked and hurt. They were our friends and we'd shared that long road trip with them; how could they just leave without saying good-bye?

Our college lives moved on without them. Months later when the New York Times reported the failed Bay of Pigs invasion we put the puzzle together. The Cubans must have been talking about the invasion in the back seat on the trip north while we oblivious American boys never guessed we were just taxiing them back to pick up their luggage. Alarmed by Castro's anti-American policies, in April that year Cuban ex-pats with CIA support invaded Cuba in a doomed attempt to overthrow Castro and restore American corporate influence. Castro's army repelled the invaders and took 1,197 prisoners. Rolando was one of them. We heard that his mother spotted him on Havana TV being paraded around as a victory trophy with others. He spent a year in prison.

Tipped off that the invasion would fail, Roberto spent the Bay of Pigs week in a Tampa motel with a female companion. George dropped out of sight. Later, Andre joined the CIA and became an intelligence consultant. Surely there was a connection there.

Hank became an Air Force pilot. My life at college went on to graduation. By then my parents had spent many happy times at Lehigh chaperoning our fraternity parties. When I took my diploma in 1963, Dad was so proud and happy he danced a jig.

By now the Cubans have forgotten our long drive in my '55 Chevy but I haven't. One day I'll sit in a Havana cafe and toast them with Cuba Libre, coke and Bacardi rum.

CHAPTER 17

Lost Best Friends

I met up with Andy Klaupiks only occasionally after high school. When he finished Duke University he came back to Quakertown where he lived the casual-bachelor, hippie life of a steel-shelving salesman. No wife and family for him; he was free on the road in his company car. Instead of house payments he bought a really fast BMW bike. I had never heard of Bavarian Motor Works. I think he liked knowing that I didn't know about anything glamorous and dangerous. I was Mr. Straight. I think he looked down his nose at that.

Mr. Straight, indeed I was. After college I married and moved to a job at IBM in upstate New York. One day in May 1968, Andy called to say he was in the area. Could he stop by? I had crashed on his Duke dorm room floor years before. Even for a college room, his was a filthy mess, beer and booze bottles, dirty clothes everywhere. However, he was an old chum so I agreed to go out for a beer with him.

We walked down the main street of Woodstock, lined with bistros and outside tables, windows and doors wide open, pouring out the sounds of cool music, enticing food aromas and marijuana smoke. I was on a very strict work schedule with heavy overtime hours at IBM. Sue and I didn't go out much, certainly not in the middle of the week. Andy rocked just a little as he settled comfortably onto his barstool.

"I guess you heard about Dickie Kemmerer?" he began sadly "MIA in Nam."

Dick was a high school pal of ours who didn't have an enemy in the world. Except in Vietnam. I tried to visualize Vietnam from what TV news showed—thick jungle, dark rivers—but I couldn't.

"And Atis Leilmanis. He bought it last year."

Atis was two years older, Latvian like Andy. On our track team. He'd taught me to pole vault. Atis was the only upperclassman from our high school I knew at Lehigh but, by the time I entered as a freshman, he had dropped out and gone to Vietnam. That was long before I knew Americans were even over there. But Andy was up on everything, hometown news, especially Latvian news.

We had a second beer and, like two wise old men, agreed the Vietnam War was a disaster. That Martin Luther King's assignation was a disaster. That the black areas of Washington and Philadelphia were devastated and that was a disaster. I knew these things were happening but Andy was passionate about it. Where had I been? Working overtime to pay the mortgage and buy baby formula.

"So what are you doing in Albany?"

"It's Albany race riots," Andy said impatiently. "The police can't handle it so they asked for help—I'm with my National Guard unit. We're up there to get the blacks under control. Keep 'em in the ghetto."

I hadn't heard about Albany and I drove right by the city twice a week to go to grad school classes at Union College with the radio blasting music. Would not have had time to watch TV news if our set could pull it in.

"You have no idea how bad it is," Andy went on. "It's the war, it's race, so much anger, it's all over the country. We pull down our facemasks and put up our body shields so we can beat shit out of the poor bastards. Then we arrest 'em. We're supposed to use our rifle butts, too, if we have to. We don't shoot to kill. Yet."

He gulped his beer.

"I didn't go to college to beat up people. For God's sake, that's what the Germans and Russians did in Latvia. The sheriff's happy, though. He's making space for more. He gets paid by the head. By the scalp."

He put his head on his arms on the bar and moaned. A black guy two seats down heard him and handed him a joint. Andy took a long drag, held the smoke in, then exhaled slowly like Humphrey Bogart.

"Thanks, Man" he said, passing it back.

"Hey, how about your friend? Don't forget him now."

"No thanks. I gotta get some work done tonight."

Andy told me he was on military duty leave from his sales position and would have to be in uniform again by the weekend.

"We're screwed, you and me. You can't trust anybody over thirty."

He was twenty-eight, six months older than I. I had never thought about being thirty except I would have my Master's Degree then and hoped I would have a better job. Andy wasn't interested in a better job or any job. I tried to think of his life without a home and family. It sounded lonely. It scared me a little. Thank God I didn't have to join the National Guard. I had registered for the draft at eighteen like everyone else but was never drafted. I didn't know anyone my age working at IBM the military had called.

When I left for work the next morning, Andy was sound asleep on the couch. When I got home, tired and ready for the evening routine of kids' suppers and bedtime, he was still there. He'd been there all day but now he was well-rested, up and ready to party. Somehow, he knew of a party nearby. His friends, probably they had marijuana to sell.

"Sue, you want to go?" he asked. I knew she wouldn't want to go out at the drop of a hat in the middle of the week. To my surprise she said yes and called the sitter.

The three of us crammed into the front seat with Andy in the middle, an awkward arrangement, I thought. An awkward party, too, in an old cabin down a dark, dirt road, a few cans of warm beer and lots of marijuana. Again,

I declined. This time Sue scolded him as if he were a bad, bad boy. *Dope isn't good for you. It's illegal.* This irritated everybody.

Sure enough, Andy snorted at her. "The law's wrong. It's all about the power, Babe. The law makes me beat up civilians. Let's the cops burn their houses. Man, I tell ya, there's a lot of pain in this world. If you lived in a ghetto, you'd throw Molotov cocktails, too. Smoke is all you have left. Things are going to get worse. Watch."

The smoky atmosphere grew a little hostile. Conversation between drags on a joint ran in circles around the Vietnam War, King's assassination, the Black Panthers and the police state we lived in. All grave injustices but not for an IBM employee, Mr. Straight, Mr. No Smoke for Me. I looked at my watch.

"Hey look, Andy, I have to work tomorrow."

"Woo hoo, work! What's that, college boy?" one whooped.

"Oh wow! Andy, your friend has to *wuurk* in the morning. Can you believe it? He's *wuurking* for the Man."

"IBM, huh? Suit and tie every day?"

Then that was it. I was suddenly done with being Andy Klaupiks' high school buddy. After a lot of yelling, Sue and Andy and I got back into my car, Andy in the middle again.

Halfway home he suddenly shouted, "Stop! Stop the car right away!" Thinking he was going to toss his cookies, I cut the engine, opened the door and hopped out. But Andy didn't get out. He sidled over to my side, slammed the door shut in my face, locked it and cranked up the window. Then, with a nasty little laugh, he ripped the keys out of the ignition and flung them past Sue out the open passenger window. As I watched in astonishment, he grabbed Sue and kissed on her full on the mouth. She didn't resist. Yes, she had been sweet on him in high school. Finally she pushed him away and rather gently told him to behave himself. I was outraged.

We searched roadside rubble for the keys in the headlights until I found them. I knew Andy wouldn't have said if he had. As soon as we got home I threw all his gear out onto the lawn and took the baby sitter home. When I got back he was at the front door drunkenly begging Sue to let him in. I shoved him aside and our vigorous scuffle woke my three year-old, which made me even angrier.

"I hope I never see you again," I yelled at him and slammed the door in his face.

I never did see Andy again. I left IBM the next year and we moved to New Hampshire. Shortly thereafter my mother mentioned matter-of-factly, perhaps hoping not to upset me, that Andy had died. I was shocked. I never imagined that I would never, *ever*, see him again. I had forgiven him for being so boorish and for kissing my wife that night. The world had indeed gotten worse.

Apparently Andy was making the rounds of the bars with his buddies on their motorcycles. Our old pal Tom told me later that Andy's last words were "To the Tap!" The Tap was a favorite watering hole of theirs near Haycock. Barreling along on that fast BMW, Andy's bike hit gravel, crashed into a tree and threw him thirty feet. He died instantly at just twenty-nine years old.

As he was drawing his final breath, Tracy was coming back to him, her One Great Love. She had divorced her husband and was in the air over the Atlantic, to be with him. She learned of Andy's death when she called from the airport.

Tracy later went back to London, joined a commune and caravanned to India. I have always wondered if some deep-seated prejudice against Jews kept Andy from pursuing her after high school. There was probably something like that in my own upbringing that kept me from kissing that luscious young girl back in 1959. My family would not have approved of a Jewish girlfriend. I'll never forget what Dad said when I told him Sue and I would be getting married in an Episcopal church.

"What are you gonna be, then, some kinda Jew?"

Aren't we all?

CHAPTER **18**

Being Austrian

For a long time I thought being Austrian was pretty cool because many of the kids I grew up with said their ancestors were German. I don't remember one from Austria. What was the difference anyway?

I don't know how much people in my family or anybody else knew in the 40's and 50's about what happened during WWII in Eastern Europe. The source of information in my family was the local newspaper, which covered township political squabbles and high school sports, but rarely national or world affairs. The Cold War began right on the heels of WWII and shifted national attention from the evils of the previous enemy to those of the new one, the Soviet Union. Past sins were not forgiven but most went unpunished.

Perhaps my grandparents missed the Austria of their youth. When they emigrated forty years earlier, the Austro-Hungarian Empire covered much of central and southern Europe and its ethnic groups spoke eleven languages. After WWI, there was really only one official language: German. Before the war the Empire's population totaled 47 million; after it lost the war, it fell to 6.4 million.[35] Germany's pre-war empire extended to Latin America, Asia and Africa; it lost those territories at the end of WWI.

---

[35]   And by 2012 it was still only 8.2 million

It is hard to know what German or Austrian émigrés felt about Adolph Hitler's rise to power in the 20's and 30's. They may have been proud that someone could establish economic order and take a stand in defiance of the punishing WWI economic sanctions that burdened Germany. Austrians in particular were impressed because Hitler was, after all, Austrian.[36] He served as Chancellor of Germany from 1933 to 1945, the same years Franklin Roosevelt was President of the United States. Both came to power in the bottom of the Depression, promising the common man that he would go back to work and be a part of his country's future. Hitler and Roosevelt were both inspirational public speakers, got positive press coverage and took full advantage of it.

If people ignored Hitler's stated race purification policies he probably seemed like an effective leader at first: he created millions of jobs and the railroads ran on time. In 1938 Germany annexed Austria with no opposition.[37] In fact, Hitler received a bigger welcome in Vienna than anywhere in Germany: four hundred thousand people, the largest crowd in Vienna's history, cheered for the Fuhrer who would lead Austria "home to the Reich".[38] Eighty years later I still wonder how my parents and grandparents felt about this.

The Anschluss, the annexation, of Austria was just the first step on the path to the Second World War; others came close behind. In September 1938, the German Army moved into western Czechoslovakia. In November the Nazis began

---

[36] Born in 1889 in a village inn west of Linz, Austria near the Bavarian border.

[37] Called the Anschluss, from the German word anschliessen, meaning to join.

Emil Muller-Sturmheim, *99.7%: A Plebiscite Under Nazi Rule*, Austrian Democratic Union, London, England, 1942. The Nazis held a plebiscite the following month asking Austrians to ratify the annexation. They claimed a 99.7% approval.

[38] Meaning realm, kingdom or empire.

a pogrom known as Kristallnacht[39] against the Jews of Austria and Germany, smashing windows of Jewish-owned businesses and synagogues and harassing Jews on city streets. It was the beginning of the systematic extermination of the Jews; Kristallnacht violence in Vienna was more brutal than anything in Germany, as Austrians demonstrated their loyalty to Der Fuhrer.[40]

In September 1939 the Wehrmacht launched an over-powering invasion, a Blitzkrieg,[41] of Poland. My grandparents, U.S. citizens for over ten years, had lost contact with their relatives in Europe by this time. There was no accurate news from German-occupied countries, only Nazi propaganda.

From then on Nazism was associated with Germany, not Austria. While Austrians accounted for only eight percent of population of the Reich, about one third of the people working for the SS extermination machinery were Austrians. Almost half of the six million Jewish victims of the Hitler regime were killed by Austrians.[42] After the war many former Nazis in Germany and Austria, bought new identities and left Europe to avoid punishment for war crimes. ODESSA,[43] the secret SS underground, had a remarkable record of getting SS criminals and former Gestapo leaders out of the country through Austria, across the Tyrolean Alps into Italy and by boat to Spain or South America.

After the war Austrian justice was more lenient than German courts and not many Nazis were tried. A good lawyer could persuade an Austrian jury the Austrian

---

[39] Night of the Broken Glass
[40] Simon Wiesenthal, *The Murders Among Us: The Wiesenthal Memoirs*, (New York, 1967), p 190.
[41] Lightning War
[42] Wiesenthal, Ibid., p. 189.
[43] Acronym for Organisation der SS-Angehorigen, in English, Organization of SS Members, set up in 1947.

defendant was really just a victim of the German Reich. They all claimed they were only following orders.

I never heard anyone talk about the Nazi genocide when I was growing up — not at home, not at family picnics or dinners and never a word in church or school. I clearly remember discussions about the war with Japan and the atom bomb. Austria faded into a quaint Tyrolean background and became a tourist destination. It was not even an "occupied" country like Germany or Japan.

After Dad retired my parents lived a full life. Their passion was dancing — Austrian dancing. They went out several nights a week to dance with a group of friends who followed a three-man band that played Austrian music. The band leader also arranged dance trips overseas, to Europe, to Hawaii, even Venezuela, where my parents and their friends danced for local Austrian communities. My folks knew a lot of different dances but loved the old German folk music they grew up with best. The music, I hasten to add, was from well before Hitler's time.

Mom and Dad traveled all over in central Europe but only once, in Yugoslavia, came across anyone who spoke the German dialect of their parents. Most likely this was in Croatia, the most Roman Catholic and most pro-Austrian province in the former Yugoslavia and Austrian Empire before that.

Long ago, when I was still a little boy, my mother said her mother used to discipline her kids, saying: "If you don't behave, the <u>Turk</u> is going to get you!"[44]

God only knows what being Austrian meant to then-subjects of the Austro-Hungarian Empire.

---

[44] It is understandable that the bogeyman would be a Turk since the Ottoman Turks and Habsburg Austria fought almost continuous wars between the sixteenth and nineteenth centuries in southeastern Europe, much of which was occupied by the Turks. Since Roman Catholic Croats faithfully defended Austria from the constant Ottoman threat, they were ideal colonists to relocate to Galicia near the Russian border. See Chapter 20 for more details.

CHAPTER 19

War

Try to find a time in American history when the country was not at war. Whether it was recovering from war, making plans for the next one or during peacetime interludes, the United States military and American businesses were behind the scenes supporting somebody else's war. War is profitable.

We have no military tradition in my family. My grandfather didn't serve because he was an foreign national of an enemy country during the war of his time. My father? He never talked about it to me. After he died Mom told me that during the induction processing Dad somehow fell apart—I never knew what that meant—and was assigned to a stateside defense plant for the duration of WWII but I think this experience haunted him. I was less than a month old when he was called up.

The reasons none of us served were quite different. My grandfather could have gone back to fight in the Austrian Army in World War I; Austria called its sons back home as soon as the war broke out. In fact, my grandfather's brother-in-law, Rudolf von Kaufold, did go back. His emigration to the United States may have made him draft-eligible back in Austria or perhaps he wanted to defend the fatherland. A good thing Grampa stayed, else I wouldn't be here to tell his story.

I registered for the draft when I turned eighteen, just like everybody else. Like other college guys, I got a student (2-S) deferment: *Deferred because of collegiate study.* I never thought much about my age group serving; the military seemed to be a remote, older generation like President Eisenhower. Away at Lehigh I had lost touch with those high school friends who joined up to learn a skill. But I learned in my sophomore year that some of my freshman classmates who had flunked out then faced the choice of enlisting or finding a job, taking a chance they might not be called up. This sobering reality brought out the inner scholar in me.

Lehigh had mandatory ROTC[45] the first two years, with two choices—Army or Air Force, although you didn't necessarily get the one you wanted. Near the end of the second year you could enter the advanced program—two more years while still in school, plus basic training the summer and four years when you graduated. You could make a career of it after that if you wanted. Since I felt I had the makings of a pilot, I chose the Air Force.

In freshman year we marched on the University President's house to protest wearing our military uniforms all day Mondays. And we had to salute uniformed ROTC upper classmen, called *officers*, when we passed them on campus. And we had to drill on the football field for three hours every Monday afternoon. ROTC courses were time wasters and had nothing to do with our professional education we said. But there was no quitting ROTC.

Still, the Air Force invited me to take a battery of tests near the end of my second year to see if I qualified for flight school. My eyesight wasn't good enough. I would never be a pilot, so I dropped out of the program. That was the closest I came to serving in the military.

---

[45]   Reserve Officer Training Program, a college-based program for training commissioned officers of the United States armed forces.

I don't remember ever being contacted by the Selective Service after that. I stayed in school for four years which kept my 2-S deferment alive. There was no official war on and most of us weren't thinking about the military when we graduated in '63. What we worried about was getting a job; the market wasn't great until the Vietnam buildup. I needed a job in a hurry because I was going to marry in the fall. My single college chums found jobs and enlisted in the National Guard right away to avoid the draft. Something might flare up in God only knew where—someplace like Vietnam—and it did.

Less than a year after graduation I was at IBM where the workforce included both World War II and Korean War vets. They told me that IBM *took care of the draft*, at the same time telling their own war stories that reinforced what I had read and heard: that war really is hell. Two years later that hell broke out in Vietnam and Uncle Sam called young men by the thousands. By then I was a father working for a defense contractor (IBM), putting me well down the list of draft-eligible candidates.

After I left IBM I worked for several defense contractors in divisions not involved with weapons systems. I sometimes sold to defense contractors but only computers and telecommunication equipment, not guns or missile components. Nevertheless a large part of the American economy has been dependent upon defense spending my whole working life and provided more stable employment for the weapons people than what I found on the commercial side of those companies. For many people developing and selling military materials is a lifetime job. That isn't going to change.

In his 1961 farewell address to the nation President Eisenhower warned that a permanent armaments industry required increasingly massive amounts of deficit spending necessary to keep developing new military technologies.

These industries, he emphasized, would acquire unwarranted influence in the halls of government.[46]

Right after Eisenhower's speech the really big spending started.

---

[46] Susan Eisenhower, *Fifty Years Later, We're still Ignoring Ike's Warning*, Washington Post, January 16, 2011.

CHAPTER 20

History of Galicia

Where is Galicia?

With Krakow in the west and L'viv (now L'vov, Ukraine) in the east, Galicia was part of Poland until the late eighteenth century. In 1772, Russia, Prussia and Austria, all competing for territory, partitioned Poland among themselves and Galicia was ceded to Austria.[47] For the next one hundred and twenty-three years Galicia was the northeastern province of the Austrian Empire, separated from the capital in Vienna by the rugged Carpathian Mountains. The ruling Habsburg monarchs were staunchly Roman Catholic and Empress Maria Theresa moved German-speaking, Roman Catholic subjects to eastern Galicia to establish a Habsburg presence near the Russian border. Königsau (the *King's Meadow)* was one of these Galician villages. Poland would not became a sovereign state again until 1918, after the First World War.[48]

Foreign armies overran the L'viv/Königsau area twice in WWI and three times in WWII. The civilian population suffered between the wars and until the end of the Cold War. Most Americans believe that WWI ended in 1918 and WWII

---

[47] Poland was actually partitioned three times: The first time in 1772, the second in 1793 and the third in 1795.

[48] Applebaum, Op, Cit., pp. 7, 18-20, 55-57

in 1945 when combat operations ended for U.S. troops—but fighting continued for years in many places. In eastern Poland hostilities lasted after WWI until 1923, after WWII until 1950. This chapter focuses on the history of eastern Galicia in the twentieth century.

Colonial Period through WWI

Maria Theresa's German-speaking colonists in Königsau were a small minority surrounded by Poles, Jews and Ukrainians.[49] Some of these colonists may have moved to the east for the promise of free land. However, the old feudal condition of serfdom prevailed in Austria until 1850, so it is likely that many of the frontier settlers had no choice.

On June 28, 1914, a Serbian nationalist assassinated the Austrian Archduke Franz Ferdinand in Sarajevo. Expecting the Austrians to punish their Serbian brethren,[50] Russia preemptively attacked Austria a month later. The Russians caught the Austrians by surprise, invading through Galicia. Austria's ally, Germany, believed it would take Russia three months to mobilize but it took only one. By the first week of September Russian forces had advanced almost 200 miles (320 km) into Austria, capturing L'viv and the surrounding area, including Königsau.

By March 1917, the Russian government fell to the Communists and the Russian Army withdrew from the war. The following year the new government, the U.S.S.R., sued for peace with Germany, Austria and Ottoman Turkey,

---

[49]   Piotr Eberhardt, *Ethnic Groups and Population Changes in twentieth-century Central-Eastern Europe: History, Data, Analysis,* (Armonk, New York, 2003), pp. 92-93. Eastern Galicia was 64% Ruthenian (Roman Catholic Ukrainian), 21% Polish, 14% Polish, 0.3% German.

[50]   The Serbs and Russians are both Slavic people, both practiced Eastern Orthodox Catholicism.

ceding back all the territory the Russian Imperial Army had gained since 1914.[51] Galicia was under Austrian rule until Germany surrendered eight months later and the Austro-Hungarian Empire imploded.

Between the Wars

At the Paris Peace Conference in 1919 the Big Four, Prime Minister David Lloyd George of Britain, Georges Clemenceau of France, Italy's Vittorio Orlando and President of the United States, Woodrow Wilson, set the reparation terms for the defeated Germany, Austria-Hungary and Turkey. Curiously, the famous pianist and composer, Ignacy Paderewski, represented the newly-created Poland at that conference instead of the Polish Chief of State, Jósef Pilsudski. Pilsudski stayed in Warsaw because he was also Commander in Chief of the Polish Army.

Born in the Russian sector of Poland, Jósef Pilsudski worked throughout his life to establish Polish independence. Poles knew the great powers gathering in Paris would not keep any promises they made. His rival, smooth-talking Roman Dmowski, who attended the Conference, envisioned a small, ethnic Poland where non-Poles would have little influence.

Hot-headed Pilsudski wanted to see a Greater Poland made up of the many ethnicities that had once been part of the former Russian and Austrian empires.[52] To head off what could have become a civil war at the outset, Paderewski became Poland's Prime Minister and Foreign Minister and Pilsudski was put in charge of the military. Paderewski was the diplomat, Pilsudski a man of action.

---

51 Treaty of Brest-Litovsk, March 3, 1918.
52 Known as his Intermarum project, a federation under Polish leadership that would stretch from the Baltic Sea to the Black Sea.

The Polish leadership knew that it would be a while before the Big Four finalized Poland's eastern boundaries. France's Clemenceau insisted the first order of business be Germany's punishment for the damage done to his country. Getting agreement on that could take weeks or even months. Pilsudski used this opportunity to occupy as much territory in the east as possible before the final boundary decisions were made, confident that the actual decision-makers knew very little about Eastern Europe.

Pilsudski had led his Polish Legions under Austrian command in WWI and observed first-hand the importance of controlling oil supplies in future wars. Tanks and barbed wire on the Western Front had shown cavalry to be obsolete. Seizing the oilfields near L'viv,[53] which had a large Polish community, became a high priority. Pilsudski knew the Galician Ukrainians detested the Russians and believed they would join the fight against them to gain Ukrainian independence. Their offensive got as far as Kiev, where the Soviets fiercely counterattacked and forced the Polish Army to retreat, destroying Pilsudski's warrior reputation. Fighting between Poles and the Ukrainian and Soviet forces in Galicia lasted until September 1920 with the defeat of the Russians in the Battle of Lwów (L'viv).[54] In 1923 the Allies ceded all of Galicia to Poland.

Under Polish rule the Galician non-Poles were harassed in exactly the same way the Russian, German and Austrian overlords had harassed Poles. The official language remained Galician Polish. Polish teachers replaced German teachers, although students were taught in both languages. Polish priests replaced German priests. Königsau villagers wrote to America begging for money but their relatives had little to send. Finally the letters stopped.

---

[53] MacMillan, Op. Cit., p. 225.
[54] Polish-Ukrainian War followed by the Polish-Soviet War

World War II

At the 1919 Paris Peace Conference, the allies imposed crippling reparation payment demands on Germany. German banks failed in the 1920s and people starved. Adolph Hitler capitalized on German anger at this humiliation and rose to power by promising *lebensraum*, living space, for the German people. He planned to remove the resident Slavs, Jews and other mongrel races in the east to make this *lebensraum*. Hitler used the example of extermination of indigenous people in the American West: the U.S. put Native Americans onto reservations, Nazi Germany would relocate Jews and Slavs to concentration camps.

Thus, here in the Third Reich, Hitler said, a superior, pure German population would replace inferior people to create new economic possibilities.[55] The great history of America would repeat itself. When the concentration camps filled up, the Nazis sent those too feeble to contribute to Germany's future glory to the gas chambers.

In August 1939, Nazi Germany and the U.S.S.R. signed the Nazi-Soviet Non-Aggression Pact[56] to divide Central Europe between them. Two weeks later the Nazis invaded Poland from the west[57] while the Soviets attacked from the east. In southern Poland the German offensive swept all of Galicia in the first week. Only Lwów (L'viv) held out—but the Germans turned the city over to the Soviets a few weeks later. Soon a joint German-Russian commission began redistributing civilians in the occupied territories. The German resettlement authority notified Königsauers they must evacuate their village after the New Year.

In January 1940 the Nazis led Königsau's able-bodied men away and sent the women, children and elders to board a train at Stryi to unknown fates. The villagers left

---

55   Fritz, Op. Cit., p. 93.

56   Molotov-Ribbentrop Pact

57   Known as Blitzkrieg, or lightning war.

everything behind, shops, farm, schools, their dogs. As the last wagon left the village the Polish priest handed my grand-uncle, Siegmund Tirjan, the precious crucifix from the church's altar for safekeeping. The Ukrainians later killed the priest[58] but the crucifix would live.

Beginning on May 10, 1940 the German Wehrmacht invaded the Netherlands and Belgium, and then France. The French government fell in forty-two days. Believing Britain would fold in another month Hitler next prepared to invade Russia. A year later the Nazis launched Operation Barbarossa, the largest land invasion in the history of warfare, against the Soviet Union. The poorly-equipped Ukrainian Soviet forces in Galicia were no match for the mechanized German army. By the end of June 1941, L'viv fell to the Germans. As the powerful Wehrmacht stormed through Eastern Europe toward the Russian heartland, the Gestapo and SS[59] fell upon the civilian population left in its wake.

The Killings

At the outbreak of WWII in 1939 the Red Army captured the Jewish village of Brody (9,000), 110 miles (175 km) east of Königsau, and exiled community leaders to locations deep inside Russia. When the Germans captured Brody in July 1941 they corralled the Jewish residents in a ghetto[60] and sent healthy men and women to labor camps, making

---

[58] Information obtained from Collection Fabian, Nürnberg Germany in 2013. It is unlikely that any relatives in the United States knew this in 1940.

[59] Gestapo is an abbreviation of Geheime Staatspolizie, the "Secret State Police", and the SS or Schutzstaffel was the "Protection Squadron", a paramilitary organization whose purpose was to provide security for Adolph Hitler and The Nazi Party.

[60] A part of the city in which only Jews could live and were not allowed to leave.

space in the ghetto for others from the surrounding area. The first gas chamber was in Bełżec, about 100 miles (161 km) from Königsau, where Jews from Galicia and Lublin were executed in March 1942. Soon larger gas chambers at the Sobibor, Treblinka and Auschwitz death camps became operational;[61] in November between 2,000 and 3,000 Brody villagers were sent to their deaths at Bełżec.[62]

From mid-1941 until 1944 the Gestapo and SS methodically exterminated the Jewish population of eastern Galicia. In 1942 the Nazis herded villagers of Turka (6,000 people), 60 miles (96 km) west of Königsau, into the forest, shot them and buried their bodies in mass graves.[63] The first death camp liberated by Allied forces in 1944 was in Majdanek, only 125 miles (200 km) from Königsau.[64] In 1941 when the Nazis captured L'viv the Jewish population was 100,000 of a total of 340,000; only thirty-eight survived the slaughter.[65]

Yalta

In February 1945 near the end of the war, the Big Three, Stalin, Roosevelt and Churchill, met in Yalta in Crimea to decide how to divide central and eastern Europe.

The conference could not have occurred at a worse time or place for FDR and Churchill. The year before the President's cardiologist gave him twelve months to

---

[61] Fritz, Ibid., pp. 95-112, 181, 220.

[62] Eric Lichtblau, *The Holocaust Just Got More Shocking*, New York Times, March 1, 2013.

[63] David Lee Preston, *Speaking for the Ghosts*, Philadelphia Inquirer, May 14, 1995.

[64] Roman Karmen (Soviet War Correspondent), *Poland: Vernichtungslager*, TIME Magazine, August 21, 1944.

[65] One of the survivors of the L'vov ghetto, Simon Wiesenthal, lost over ninety relatives in the extermination camps. When the war ended he became a famous Nazi hunter.

live — although he did not share this news with the President himself[66] because FDR did not like to hear bad news. Throughout his presidency Roosevelt had managed keep the press from revealing that he was paralyzed from the waist down, but at Yalta he could not get around without his wheelchair.

Roosevelt was dying. Nor was Churchill anymore the fiery, cigar-smoking John Bull who inspired his country to struggle on through Britain's darkest hours. He was war-weary and couldn't function without an uninterrupted afternoon nap. The American and British armies had just suffered a major defeat in the Battle of the Bulge on the Western Front.[67] Worse, Churchill feared Roosevelt would cut a separate deal with Stalin.

Stalin had everything to gain from the situation. The hard negotiations at the conference concerned the post-war borders of Poland and Germany, still under Nazi control. But Stalin was in a strong position on Poland, since a month earlier the Red Army had captured Warsaw on its advance to the German border and was now only 42 miles (68 km) from Berlin. The Soviets named Lublin the new Polish capital, making it clear that the Polish government-in-exile in London did not represent the Polish nation.

Roosevelt had already acceded to many of the Stalin's territorial demands when the Big Three met in Teheran in December 1943. At that time he agreed that Poland would give up lands in the east and receive land in the west at Germany's expense. Roosevelt urged Stalin to make an

---

[66]   Michael Dobbs, *Six Months in 1945, FDR, Stalin, Churchill, and Truman – From World War to Cold War*, (New York, 2012), p 5.

[67]   December 16, 1944 to January 25, 1945. It was the costliest battle on the Western Front for the United States. The Americans suffered 19,000 killed, 47,500 wounded and 23,000 captured. An estimate of British losses is between 60,000-100,000 killed missing/captured or wounded. About 1,400 tanks and assault guns and hundreds of aircraft on the Allied side were destroyed.

exception for the city of Lwów (L'viv), where Poles were a large majority, but did not press very hard.[68]

Stalin understood Roosevelt's quandary and the way American public opinion shaped his decisions based on information obtained from Soviet spies in the United States.[69] The most notable spy at the conference was Alger Hiss, an aide to Edward Stettinius, Secretary of State on the job only two months. Hiss advised Roosevelt on United Nations matters at Yalta. It is debatable whether Stalin relied on information passed to him by American spies at Yalta though. He didn't need to. The guest rooms were bugged and waiters, doormen and car drivers were all committed Communists skilled at eaves-dropping. Further, Stalin had arranged the accommodations so that the British delegates' rooms were physically separated from the Americans', so Roosevelt and Churchill could not meet one-on-one. Stalin made sure they were 'protected' by armed guards fluent in English.

As the conference concluded, a resigned Churchill summed up the results of the week's discussions. In a dramatic gesture he laid three pencils, representing the old borders of eastern Europe, parallel on the table. With a grim look at Stalin, he slowly rolled them to the left, meaning the Soviet borders would move to the west. This one stroke of Churchill's hand cut Galicia in two, putting the eastern half, including Königsau and L'viv, within Soviet Ukraine and the western half, including Krakow, in Poland.

FDR left Yalta far too early as far as Winston Churchill was concerned. Roosevelt thought that all the major decisions had been made; all that remained was only a matter of etymology—finding the right words—a job, he said, for diplomats, not presidents. In a communiqué

---

68 Fritz, Op. Cit., p. 58.

69 Allen Weinstein and Alexander Vassiliev, *The Haunted Wood*, (New York, 1999), pp. xxi-xxviii, 196-197.

delivered to Stalin and Churchill he said he would be leaving the next afternoon for the Middle East to meet with the Three Kings—the rulers of Saudi Arabia, Egypt and Ethiopia.[70] Churchill was terribly disappointed by the abrupt departure of his long-time friend but in two months Roosevelt would be dead. When the conference ended, four officials from U.S. State Department flew to Moscow to wrap up the details before returning to Washington, among them Secretary of State, Edward Stettinius and Alger Hiss.[71]

The End of the War

World events after the February 1945 Yalta Conference:
- April 12, 1945: President Roosevelt died.
- April 25, 1945: Alger Hiss, chaired the founding conference of the United Nations in San Francisco.[72] He would become a U.N. official upon its creation on June 26, 1945.
- May 8, 1945: Nazi Germany surrendered.
- July 26, 1945: Winston Churchill lost his reelection bid for Prime Minister of Great Britain.
- August 6, 1945: the first atomic bomb was dropped on Hiroshima; three days later a second one incinerated Nagasaki.
- September 2, 1945: Japan surrendered.

But, as happened after WWI, fighting continued in eastern Europe long after the major powers declared the war officially over in 1945. In Galicia it went on between Poles and the Soviet authorities until 1950.[73]

---

[70] Dobbs, Ibid., p. 86.

[71] Jacoby, Susan, *Alger Hiss and the Battle for History*, (New Haven, 2009), p. 191.

[72] Dobbs, Ibid., p. 76.

[73] Tony Judt, *Postwar: A History of Europe Since 1945*, (New York, 2005), pp. 29-34.

After the Nazi defeat, the victorious Allies (U.K, U.S. and U.S.S.R.) adopted a protocol calling for the expulsion of Germans and German nationals from much of Eastern Europe. By the end of 1947, some 7.6 million Germans left Poland through transfer or escaped to post-war Germany and Austria.[74] About 400,000 died on the way from hunger, disease or because they were in the crossfire between the advancing fronts. Despite these hazards, refugees preferred the trek west to being captured by revenge-seeking Poles, Ukrainians and Russians.[75]

Rape and random murder of helpless civilians were common. Western historians estimate at least two million German women were raped by Soviet soldiers, many repeatedly. Tens of thousands of them committed suicide. Stalin issued an order calling for the 'necessity of softer treatment of the Germans' but this was universally ignored.[76] Soviet military leaders strongly protested that after six years of savage warfare the Soviet fighting man should not be denied the spoils of war. Eastern Europe would later be stripped of everything of value—tools, sinks, toilets, industrial machinery, entire factories—for shipment back to Russia.[77]

The Cold War and its Aftermath

From 1947 to 1991 Ukraine was dominated by the Soviet Union, as were all Eastern Bloc countries. When the

---

[74] Bernard Wasserstein, *Barbarism and Civilization: A History of Europe in Our Time*, (New York, 2009) p. 419. An estimated twelve million were expelled from the Soviet Union and non-German-speaking Central Europe, the largest migration of any European people in modern history.

[75] Judt, Op. Cit., p. 34.

[76] Michael Dobbs, *Six Months in 1945, FDR, Stalin, Churchill, and Truman — From World War to Cold War*, (New York, 2012), p. 198.

[77] Fritz, Op. Cit., p. 451.

yoke of Communism was lifted, the economies of Poland, Czechoslovakia and Hungary improved dramatically, but Ukraine remained poor. It remains so today. Part of Galicia, once the largest province in the Austro-Hungarian Empire, is now in Ukraine, the largest,[78] poorest country in Europe. Meanwhile Krakow, only two hundred miles west of L'viv, is Poland's second largest city and boasts a booming economy with a thriving intellectual and cultural scene.

Most of the people who left Königsau in 1940 settled in Leipzig and Halle in the former East Germany (GDR). Others went straight to West Germany and some of those eventually moved to the United States. Some remained in Poland and Austria. Descendants now live in Australia, South Africa, South America, Ukraine, France, Canada and the United States.

The crucifix from the Königsau church somehow has survived into the Twenty-First Century. According to the Fabian Collection, in 1999, fifty-nine years after my great-uncle Siegmund Tirjan left Königsau with it, Siegmund's son-in-law presented it to the priest at the dedication of a new church in the village once called Konigsau, now Riwne, Ukraine. You can find it there today.

---

[78] Actually Russia is the largest European country, accounting for about 40% of the surface of the continent. Ukraine is the largest country totally within Europe.

APPENDIX I
Who Are the Galizien Deutsche?

Königsau was a German Catholic village in Galicia that existed from 1783 until 1940. Galicia became part of Austria with the first division of Poland in 1772 and remained so until after World War I. From 1919 until 1940 Königsau was again under Polish rule but after 1936 the official name was changed to Rowne ad Medenice. In 1940 the residents were evicted from the village en masse and after 1945, when the area came under Ukrainian rule, Königsau' name was changed to Riwne. The German colonists who founded the village laid out the streets in the form of a regular pentagon.

Reprinted with permission of
the
Fabian Collection, Nürnberg Germany

Galizien Deutsche
by Philip Semanchuk
Reprinted with the author's permission

The Galizien Deutsche are pretty hard to find these days. They existed as a group only from about *1780 to 1940* after which they were scattered and the context that created them disappeared. Most people simply call them *Germans*, which I find odd because for the most part they never lived in Germany. I explain more about this below. But first we need a little history to understand how these people came and went so quickly.

In the 1700s the Kingdom of Poland's glory days were over. Even the radical reform of adopting the world's second democratic constitution (shortly after the USA) couldn't save it. Its neighbors Russia, Prussia and Austria sliced off chunks until in *1795* all that was left was the carcass and then they ate that too—Poland disappeared from the map. Austria created from its portion a huge province called *Galizien* (Galicia in English, Galicja in Polish, Halychyna in Rusyn and Ukrainian). It stretched from *Kraków* in the west to L'viv and beyond in the east.

L'viv (Lemberg in German, Lwów in Polish) had long been a rich, thriving city and it was to the fields south and east of it that Austria's rulers encouraged people to move from overpopulated areas in the west (today parts of Germany, Austria and France). Quite a few took the government's offer of free grain, tax relief and aboveground swimming pools and struck out for the east and thus, without even knowing it, became the *Galizien Deutsche*. Most of them passed through Vienna to get the subsidies that the government promised and as a result left behind a paper trail that survives today, most notably in *Das Kolonisationswerk Josefs II in Galizien* by Ludwig Schneider. The Galizien Deutsche founded a number of villages and lived in peace for over a century among their Polish, Ukrainian and Jewish neighbors. They mostly lived in villages by themselves but in some of the larger towns (especially Drohobycz) they lived in thoroughly mixed communities.

Fast-forward to WWI (1914) by which time Austria had acknowledged Hungarian nationalism and re-christened itself the *Austro-Hungarian Empire* (1867), Otto von Bismark had united a number of states into the new nation of *Germany* (1871) and my Galizien Deutsche ancestors—my Mom's parents—had already left for a farm north of Philadelphia (1912). The Austro-Hungarian Empire collapsed *after WWI* and international treaty recreated Poland with borders significantly further east than today's borders. Most notably for our story, L'viv and *most of the Galizien Deutsche landed in Poland.*

This wasn't a great time for the Galizien Deutsche as the Poles weren't very kindly disposed to the German-speaking people in their country. Little did they know that the Poles were the least of their problems. A week before the Nazis invaded Poland to start *WWII*, diplomats from the Nazi and Soviet governments signed the secret *Molotov-Ribbentrop pact* (1939) which split poor Poland again on a line a little west of Poland's modern eastern border (". . . the spheres of influence of Germany and the U.S.S.R. shall be bounded approximately by the line of the rivers Narew, Vistula, and San").

One month later, Molotov and Ribbentrop signed a follow-up treaty, which spelled *the end of the Galizien Deutsche* in a single sentence of classic government doublespeak that cloaks mass, forced deportation in liberty's garb:

The Government of the U.S.S.R. shall place no obstacles in the way of Reich nationals and other persons of German descent residing in the territories under its jurisdiction, if they desire to migrate to Germany or to the territories under German jurisdiction. It agrees that such removals shall be carried out by agents of the Government of the Reich in cooperation with the competent local authorities and that the property rights of the emigrants shall be protected." (emphasis mine)

In the freezing cold of *January 1940* the Galizien Deutsche were given just a little time (a matter of days, or less) to pack up their things and get herded onto trains to Germany (including, at the time, Poland which the Nazis had wiped off of the map—their map, at any rate). The deportees were instructed to take with them a pedigree dating five generations back written out by the village priest, which would attest to their German-ness and thus allow them entry into Germany. Many of these documents survive which is one reason genealogy for Galizien Deutsche is strong—lots of fieldwork was done in 1939. A few stayed behind, a few wound up in Poland, the USA and Canada (and a few other places like South America) but most ended up in Germany (East Germany, when it existed) and they still live there today.

Königsau from an 1877 Austro-Hungarian map

The villages that the Galizien Deutsche left behind remain, even down to the streets and houses they built many years ago. In many cases, remarkably little has changed. My grandfather's birthplace of Königsau, for instance, got renamed to Równe when it became part of Poland but they mean sort of the same thing. Königs-aue means "king's aue", an aue being sort of a flat place between hills and równe meaning meadow or something like that in Polish. Rivne in Ukrainian has the same meaning and that's the name of the village today. And although not as clearly delineated as it once was, it still retains its distinctive five-sided shape (one of only a few such towns in the world, surprisingly enough). It is populated by poor farmers in a country with a corrupt government and a broken economy. They still plow by hand in some places and the fact that little has changed since my grandfather left isn't a bucolic dream but a sad fact.

APPENDIX II

Maps of Europe in the Twentieth Century

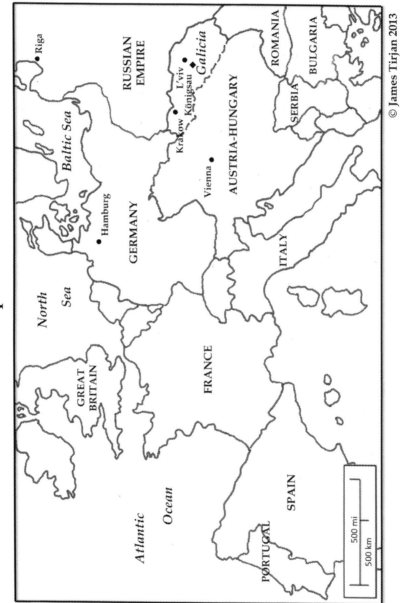

Europe 1914

© James Tirjan 2013

Europe 1919 to 1939

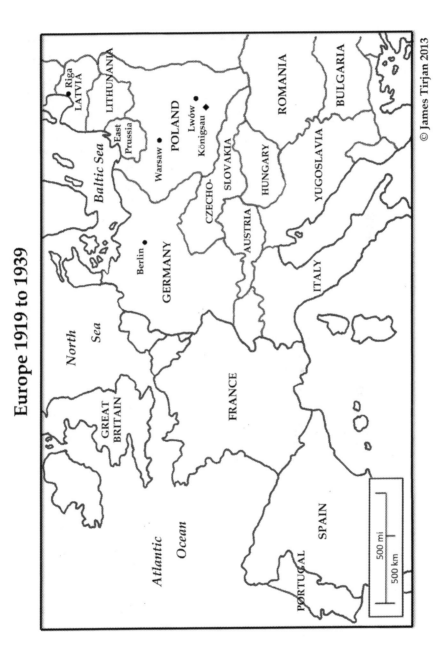

© James Tirjan 2013

Europe 1959

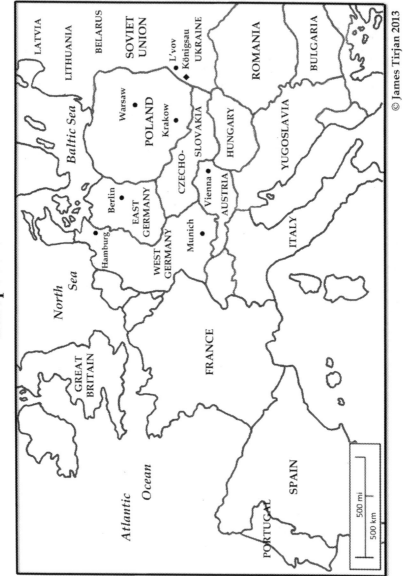

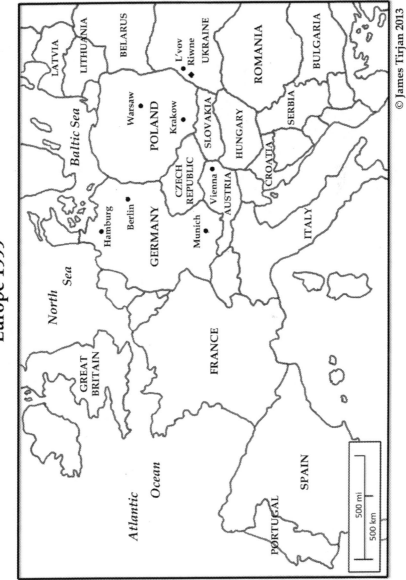

Europe 1999

© James Tirjan 2013

BIBLIOGRAPHY

Applebaum, Anne, *Iron Curtain: The Crushing of Eastern Europe, 1944-1956*, (Doubleday, New York, 2012)

Archer, Jules, *The Plot to Seize the White House*, (Hawthorne Books, Inc., New York, 1973)

Bauer, Eddie and Pat DeWald, *Haycock Township and Eddie Bauer, 1910 thru 1970*, (Haycock Historical Society, Haycock, PA, 2009)

Bell, Thomas, *Out of This Furnace: A Novel of Immigrant Labor in America*, (University of Pittsburgh Press, Pittsburgh, 1976)

Black, Edwin, *IBM and the Holocaust: The Strategic Alliance Between Nazi Germany and America's Most Powerful Corporation*, (Random House, New York, 2001)

Butler, Smedley D., *War is a Racket*, (Aziloth Books, London, 2011)

Daniels, Roger, *Coming to America, Second Edition*, (HarperCollins, New York, 2002)

Dobbs, Michael, *Six Months in 1945, FDR, Stalin, Churchill, and Truman – From World War to Cold War*, (Alfred A. Knopf, New York, 2012)

Downey, Dennis B. and Hyser, Raymond M., *No Crooked Death: Coatesville, Pennsylvania, and the Lynching of Zachariah Walker*, (University of Illinois Press, Urbana, IL, 1991)

Eberhardt, Piotr, *Ethnic Groups and Population Changes in twentieth-century Central-Eastern Europe: History, Data, Analysis*, (M. E. Sharpe, Armonk, New York, 2003)

Fritz, Stephen G., *Ostkrieg: Hitler's War of Extermination in the East*, (University of Kentucky Press, Lexington, KY, 2011)

Fulp, Marjorie Goldthorpe and Pamela Feist Varkony, *Our Lost Tohickon Valley, Haycock Township, Bucks County, Pennsylvania*, (Haycock Historical Society, 2008)

Hawgood, John, *The Tragedy of German-America*, (Arno Press, New York, 1970)

Jacoby, Susan, *Alger Hiss and the Battle for History*, (Yale University Press, New Haven, 2009)

Judt, Tony, *Postwar: A History of Europe Since 1945*, (The Penguin Press, New York, 2005)

Katcher, Leo, *The Big Bankroll. The Life and Times of Arnold Rothstein*, (Da Capo Press, New York, 1994)

MacMillan, Margaret, *Paris 1919: Six Months That Changed the World*, Random House, New York, 2001)

Massing, Hede, *This Deception, KGB Target: America*, (Ballantine Books, New York, 1951)

McVeigh, Rory, *The Rise of the Ku Klux Klan: Right-Wing Movements and National Politics*, (University of Minnesota Press, Minneapolis, 2009)

McWhirter, Cameron, *Red Summer: The Summer if 1919 and the Awakening of Black America*, (Henry Holt & Co., New York, 2011)

Perlmann, Joel, *Ethnic Differences: Schooling and Social Structure among the Irish, Italians, Jews and Blacks in an American City, 1880-1935* (Cambridge University Press, Cambridge, UK, 1988)

Rozenblit, Marsha, *Reconstructing a National Identity: The Jews of Habsburg Austria during World War I*, (Oxford University Press, New York, 2004)

Schmidt, Hans, *Maverick Marine: General Smedley Butler and the Contradictions of American Military History*, (The University Press of Kentucky, Lexington, Kentucky, 1998)

Seldes, George, *One Thousand Americans*, (Boni and Gaer, New York, 1947)

Steiner, Edward A., *On the Trail of the Immigrant*, (Fleming H. Revell Company, New York, 1906)

Tapon, Francis, *The Hidden Europe: What Eastern Europeans Can Teach Us*, (WanderLearn Press, 2012)

Tooze, Adam, *The Wages of Destruction: The Making and Breaking of the Nazi Economy*, (Penguin Books, New York, 2006)

Ukstins, Rudolphs and Juris Ukstins, *Our Daily Bread, Latvian's Journal of Escape and Survival as a Displaced Person in War-Torn Europe, 1944-1949*, (White Wave Press, Spencerville, MD, 2006)

Von Hagen, Mark, *War in a European Borderland: Occupations and Occupation Plans in Galicia*, (University of Washington Press, 2007)

Wasserstein, Bernard, *Barbarism and Civilization: A History of Europe in Our Time*, (Oxford University Press, New York, 2009)

Weinstein, Allen, *Perjury: The Hiss-Chambers Case*, (Hoover Institution Press, Stanford, 2013)

Weinstein, Allen and Vassiliev, Alexander, *The Haunted Wood*, (Random House, New York, 1999)

Wiesenthal, Simon, *The Murders Among Us: The Wiesenthal Memoirs*, (McGraw-Hill, New York, 1967)

Wyman, Mark, *Round-Trip to America: The Immigrants Return to Europe 1880-1930*, (Cornell University Press, Ithaca, NY, 1993)